Ezra Pound
and
The Pisan Cantos

Ezra Pound
and
The Pisan Cantos

by Anthony Woodward

Routledge & Kegan Paul
London, Boston and Henley

First published in 1980
by Routledge & Kegan Paul Ltd
39 Store Street, London WC1E 7DD,
9 Park Street, Boston, Mass. 02108, USA and
Broadway House, Newtown Road,
Henley-on-Thames, Oxon RG9 1EN
Set in 10/11pt Palatino by
Rowland Phototypesetting Ltd
Bury St Edmunds, Suffolk
and printed in Great Britain by
Page Bros Ltd, Norwich, Norfolk

British Library Cataloguing in Publication Data

Woodward, Anthony
Ezra Pound and 'The Pisan cantos'.
1. Pound, Ezra. Cantos, The
I. Title
811'.5'2   PS3531.082C2   79-41446

ISBN 0 7100 0372 2

To Mary de Rachewiltz

'And a modern Eleusis being possible in the wilds of a man's mind only?'

Guide to Kulchur

Contents

Acknowledgments

Princess de Rachewiltz, Ezra Pound's daughter and the author of a moving and fascinating work on her father's life, has both in personal discussion and by letter given me advice and encouragement of a kind far beyond what I had any right to expect. My colleague, Professor Brian Cheadle, made most acute and helpful suggestions, both in substance and in detail. To my wife profound gratitude is due for her encouragement and advice throughout, and for her meticulous reading of the text.

Mrs Ada Lewis has typed the manuscript in its various stages with unfailing patience and skill.

Grateful acknowledgment is made to Faber and Faber Ltd and New Directions Publishing Corporation, for permission to quote from *The Cantos* by Ezra Pound, Copyright © 1972 by The Trustees of the Ezra Pound Literary Property Trust; and to New Directions, and Peter Owen, London, for material from Ezra Pound, *Confucius*, copyright 1947 by Ezra Pound. I should also like to thank the following for permission to reproduce copyright material: Jonathan Cape Ltd, and Hill and Wang (now a division of Farrar, Straus and Giroux, Inc.), for a selection from *Writing Degree Zero* by Roland Barthes, translated from the French *Le Degré Zéro de l'Ecriture* by Annette Lavers and Colin Smith, © 1953 by Editions du Seuil, translation copyright © 1967 by Jonathan Cape Ltd; Little Brown and Company, in association with the Atlantic Monthly Press, and A. M.

Heath and Company Ltd for two extracts from *Ezra Pound Father and Teacher: Discretions* by Mary de Rachewiltz; Oxford University Press for an extract from *The Barb of Time* by Daniel Pearlman; Regnery/Gateway for an extract from a translation of Hölderlin's *Brot und Wein* which appeared in *Existence and Being* by Martin Heidegger; Viking Penguin Inc. for an extract from C. Seelye (ed.), *Charles Olson and Ezra Pound, An Encounter at St Elizabeth's,* © 1975 by the University of Connecticut.

Author's Note

Page references throughout are to *The Cantos of Ezra Pound* (Faber & Faber, London, 1975) whose pagination is the same as that of the New Directions complete edition of *The Cantos* issued in the United States. There is no line numbering in any edition of *The Cantos*. I have provided certain long passages with my own line references for the reader's convenience, and all line references in the text refer to my quoted passages.

Introduction

Whoever loves Pound's poetry, whatever its inequalities, and whoever admires the man, whatever his flaws, must have felt that there is still something equivocal about his standing. The poetic achievement is of such a major kind, yet it has not attained that accepted place in the minds of educated readers which the poetry of an Eliot or a Yeats has done. Other poets admire extravagantly the choiceness of Pound's rhythms, but this may only darken the already arcane associations of his name. Hence he becomes the possession either of adulatory cliques or of the graduate researcher and the specialist scholar. Often his wider fame is ensured only by an occasional posthumous revelation of some piece of political intransigence, guaranteed to set tongues clicking.

If one holds, with Bernard Shaw, that all professional-isms are a conspiracy against the public, then Pound's public has been the victim of a conspiracy: a learned, devoted and – I hasten to add – a necessary conspiracy, since an adequate assessment of his work as a whole will need as its basis the learning of the specialist scholar and graduate researcher. Yet an interim appreciation that aims to bring Pound closer to the educated reader at the level of his greatest achievement, *The Pisan Cantos*, may still be worth a try. Detailed commentary has not been my chief aim. I have attempted it on occasion, but with a chastening sense of how easy it is to go wrong. What has most interested me is to convey the impression of a mood, a rhythm of feeling, which pervades much of *The Pisan Cantos* and which may also tell us something about *The Cantos* as a whole.

I think one reason why Pound's status is more elusive than that of either Yeats or Eliot is that their work achieves the kind of overall unity of effect which assuages one's natural desire for the synoptic view. To gain such a view of Pound is less easy. The economic issue, if detached from the Confucianism and neo-pagan Illuminism which were the main components of Pound's eclectic religious outlook, is a red herring. Large and over-active, it does credit to his conscience and good intentions but does not, in isolation, help the reader to grasp the elusive coherence of his achievement. Eliot's religious position, by contrast, implicit in *Gerontion* and *The Waste Land,* and gradually unfolding itself in *Ash Wednesday* and *Four Quartets,* gave a unity to his performance by locating his utterances in the still familiar context of Christian sensibility and belief, whereas Pound's more reckless self-exposure to the pressures of his historical moment eschewed any such advantage. Yeats, though having no conventional leanings towards a belief hallowed through time and tradition, still managed to style the conflicting elements of his personality by means of an Occult determinism; and the 'masterful images' of his poetry, clad in a matchless rhetoric, retain even amid the fluctuations of early, middle and late styles a certain noble simplicity of gesture, so that the donning and the doffing of Masks seem contained by a personality with a very firm psychological centre. Moreover, both Eliot and Yeats, not to mention Hardy, Wallace Stevens and Frost, managed their public careers with far greater decorum than did the febrile and ferocious Ezra, whose commitment endangered his reputation and ultimately his life. Yet it is no purpose of mine to give Pound a primacy over such poets as Yeats and Eliot on account of the more dramatically *engagé* quality of his life. It is the poetry that matters, even though I see no reason for such a cleanly surgical severance of poetry from life as purists require. Each of the three poets had his endemic flaw as an artist, a flaw rooted in temperament and hence in life: Eliot's a cerebral monotony, Yeats' a too conscious eloquence, Pound's an allusive incoherence. Each had his exalted poetic flights, and of the three I myself find Pound's the most moving. But that is no great matter. I aim merely to show where lay Pound's essential greatness and his centrality to his age – a greatness and centrality only understandable in terms of his self-exposure to the disintegrative pressures which the modern age inherited from the nineteenth century and from certain aspects of the Romantic movement.

To link Pound and Romanticism may seem paradoxical, given his vigorous role in the anti-Romantic movement of early twentieth-century modernism, so I shall now venture on a few general considerations which I hope will make it appear less so.

Even the demanding Lovejoy was disposed to concede that the one '*common* factor in a number of otherwise diverse tendencies which . . . have been termed "Romantic" ' was an excited responsiveness to diversity and individuality on the part of artists in all media, with consequent effects on European civilisation as a whole, since that responsiveness 'perhaps more than any other *one* thing has distinguished, both for better and worse, the prevailing assumptions of the mind of the nineteenth and of our own century from those of the preceding period in the history of the West'. Among the examples that Lovejoy gives of this change in outlook are 'the endeavour to reconstruct in imagination the distinctive inner life of peoples remote in time or space or in cultural condition', and the 'étalage du moi'.[1] Here Lovejoy has caught two things crucial to our understanding of Pound: historicism, and fascination with the dramas of the self. A concomitant of historicism, as Lovejoy defined it, is the awareness of our own selves as historical beings, fascinated by the interplay of our historical selves with the selves of other times and places. And such concern with the self also engenders fascinated obsession with the nuances, contradictions and, ultimately, the fluidity of that self. The two taken together, historicism and self-consciousness, account for a great deal of what is most relevant to us in nineteenth-century culture and provide perhaps the most vital link between Romanticism and the modern age.

It is possible to suggest,[2] for instance, that Browning's

attempt to write a more 'objective' type of poetry in his dramatic monologues, as distinct from the subjective mode he associated with Shelley, was a means of externalising the ambiguous fluctuations and diversities of his own awareness of self, by studying its reflections in the mirror of past historical epochs. It was an early instance of the use of 'masks' or 'personae'. Thus when, in the early twentieth century, sophisticated taste recoiled from the subjective rhetoric of a decadent Romanticism, it was not surprising to find Yeats, Eliot and Pound adopting in their various ways equivalents to the Browning dramatic monologue in order to render what was in essence still the inescapable bequest of Romanticism to modernity: absorption in the fluctuations of the self in a context of historicism.

Furthermore the historical context in which the post-Romantic self found itself was now made both more exciting and more disturbing by the array of historical and pre-historical cultures that anthropological as well as historical research was unfolding. In the absence of any belief in a plan of divine Providence, and, in the writers concerned, of any belief in the surrogate religious notion of Progress, there emerged in some of the great modernists of the early twentieth century an awareness not only of what Eliot called 'the immense panorama of futility and anarchy which is contemporary history' but also of the way in which history might be mastered by calling into service the burgeoning sciences of humanity's past. In the *Musée Imaginaire* of a rootless, eclectic but knowledgeable modernity various compensatory measures could be taken. Attempts to pattern the confusions of modern life by the self-conscious use of ancient myths, fertility rituals and heroic legends were among the most prominent, and they played a part in Pound's *Cantos* as well as in *The Waste Land* and *Ulysses*. Equally prominent not long before Pound began his career – and *The Cantos* were envisaged very early on in that career – was the Symbolist desire to construct through Art the one great Book which would transmute the confusions of historical existence into permanent aesthetic essence: 'tout au monde existe pour aboutir à un livre', as Mallarmé put it. The presence of this kind of Symbolist absolutism is clear enough in Joyce and Yeats, just as the

Symbolist colouring of Eliot's mode of expression is also familiar; yet the fact that Pound dissociated himself from Symbolism should not lead us to underestimate its importance in the background. It was not for nothing that some of his early work was steeped in the languorous imagery of Yeatsian symbolism and cultivated the rare nuances of a quasi-mystical self-consciousness; nor was it for nothing that he early (1906) aspired to write an epic thus significantly defined:

> And I see my greater soul-self bending
> Sibylwise with that great forty-year epic
> *(Scriptor Ignotus)*

The epic emerged from the poet's quite explicit concerns with the twin problems of historicism and self-consciousness – Romanticism's legacy to the twentieth century. This comes out in almost naively exhilarated fashion in the early *Histrion*,[3] and is movingly evident in the famous passage from *Gaudier-Brzeska* which runs thus:

> In the 'search for oneself', in the search for 'sincere self-expression', one gropes, one finds some seeming verity. One says 'I am' this, that, or the other, and with the words scarcely uttered one ceases to be that thing.
> I began this search for the real in a book called *Personae*, casting off, as it were, complete masks of the self in each poem. I continued in long series of translations, which were but more elaborate masks.[4]

In those lines there speaks the Angst-ridden post-Romantic Self seeking Unity of Being in the context of modern historicism, with a typically ironic self-consciousness in the inverted commas that bracket 'search for oneself'. Let us next follow some of the windings of that self-consciousness in its encounter with history.

A few years after he had written that passage of *Gaudier-Brzeska* Pound issued the first version of Cantos 1–3, in the form of Browningesque soliloquy, later in its turn to be discarded in favour of the more impersonal form of mask, pastiche and translation that we now know.[5] Let us note, however, the type of emphasis that emerges at the beginning of 'Ur-Canto' 1, in the course of Pound's justifying the free form with which he was experimenting:

>   . . . and that the modern world
> Needs such a rag-bag to stuff all its thought in

The contents of 'the modern world' uppermost in Pound's mind were not, as one might conceivably have anticipated, the responses provoked by the dismal heterogeneity of the modern urban landscape, or something of that kind, nor even the confusing psychological pressures of the age (though those are hinted at in one or two lines) but the disturbing diversity of the modern artist's historical awareness, and his difficult, self-conscious relationship to history. Can he really grasp the past in its essence? Does he distort it by the imposition of his own 'Phantastikon'? Does it matter if he does? 'What have I of this life?' Pound asks.

We should also note, for the sake of its bearing on *The Cantos* proper, the kind of historical experience that obsessed the poet, feeling as he did both its kinship and its tantalising distance: ancient rituals, numinous beings, and stories where the erotic is endowed with a quasi-religious intensity. (Pound's views on the persistence in Troubadour love of an underground mystical tradition stemming from pagan mysteries is well-known from his essay on 'Psychology and the Troubadours'.) It is a modern mind's receptivity to that particular kind of eclectic material from the past which fascinated the poet, along with the elusive relation of present teller to past events and persons. Thus a double nostalgia is distilled by the 'Ur-Cantos': a nostalgia for the actuality of past experience seen from one's all too local status in the present, and a nostalgia for certain types of numinous experience that seem to have been more common in the past than in the present. This is what gives an underlying note of loss to much of the 'Ur-Cantos', in spite of the occasional Browningesque heartiness of their tone. Pound was indeed, as Wyndham Lewis put it in *Time and Western Man*, 'a man in love with the past'.

The aim of *The Cantos* proper, after the early 'Ur-Cantos' had been rejected, was to make that love a positive source of analysis and reconstruction: the poet, by means of his imaginative re-creation of certain past instances of *virtù*, civility and sacred vitality, and by means of his radical diagnosis of usury as the persistent flaw in the history of the West since the Renaissance, offers himself as a guide to the future. After all, had not the composition of *Hugh Selwyn Mauberley* intervened, and had not Pound there sloughed off his 'Doppelgänger' aesthetic self, and emerged as the maker of a great constructive epic – the 'tale of the tribe'?

So runs the Authorised Version. I agree that if Pound had not made that effort he would not be the great poet and exemplary figure that he is. Robert Lowell put the matter thus: 'Pound's social credit, his Fascism, all these various things were a tremendous gain to him; he'd be a very Parnassian poet without them. Even if they're bad beliefs – and some were bad, some weren't, and some were just terrible of course – they made him more human and more to do with life, more to do with the times. They served him. Taking what interested him in these things gave him a kind of realism and life to his poetry that it wouldn't have had otherwise.'⁶ Yet to read *The Cantos* as if Pound's didactic constructive intentions were the work's true nerve of feeling is to miss a crucial poetic effect, which is one of ironic parody and disintegration, shot through with nostalgia for a lost beauty and fierce innocence. *The Cantos* depict, as Richard Pevear has put it, 'the ruin of history',⁷ through the eyes of a poet whose greatness lay in the split that existed between his ideals and reality. An eclectic, rootless being, he exposed his imaginative powers to the historicist *mêlée* available to modern culture, but the temperamental bias of the lyric poet was in constant tension with the eager activism of the reformer. Indeed, the vituperative violence of the latter, in the prose and in parts of *The Cantos*, was the symptom of some irritable compensatory drive. Some who knew Pound noted signs of this split in his personality: on the one hand dogmatic, aggressively colourful, a fiery extrovert; on the other an intensely sensitive, tender, even shy being. Fate led him to such wholeness and serenity as can be attained by such a temperament only in the very heart of loss, as can be seen in the culminating Cantos of the Pisan series. And *The Pisan*

Cantos are the great modern elegy not only of one man over his individual fate but over a whole civilised order for which he had some claim to speak.

Consider what were his greatest achievements prior to *The Cantos*: *Cathay, Homage to Sextus Propertius* and *Hugh Selwyn Mauberley*. In *Cathay* the principal note is one of loss and loneliness, of exquisitely fine response to the transience of beauty through the 'mask' of that Chinese civilisation whose poised serenity in sadness Pound catches so well; but catches with an overtone of contrivedly understated post-Romantic *Weltschmerz* that makes for a fascinating interplay of the present with the past:

> The leaves fall early this autumn, in wind.
> The paired butterflies are already yellow with August
> Over the grass in the West garden;
> They hurt me. I grow older.

In *Homage to Sextus Propertius* an involuted irony plays with its own elegancies through the mask of a character as much possessed by death as by beauty and amorous passion. And what of *Hugh Selwyn Mauberley*? Here I must risk the arbitrary assertion that I have never been convinced that Pound managed successfully to bury Mauberley in that poem, and have always felt that the greatest power of the series lies in the poet's imaginative empathy with the delicate subtleties of Mauberley's temperament, as depicted in the latter half of the poem. The utterly ravishing 'Scattered moluccas . . .' lyric, evoking the drowned Mauberley's fate, like a kind of pre-Connolly Palinurus, has for me a power that will never be entirely rationalised by the official moral of the poem. Moving swiftly from psycho-criticism to headlong diagnosis I assert that *The Cantos* is a work by Mauberley, writ very large. *The Cantos* record the struggle of Mauberley/Pound, not wholly under conscious control, to realise the tragic dimensions of his aesthetic contemplative nature. Let us see what can be done with the possibility.

Naturally there is a danger in this view of appearing to turn Pound into a mainly elegiac sensibility; it ignores the vigour, the pungency, the ferocity of *The Cantos,* let alone their didactic intent. Surely too, it will be said, the past is evoked there in an extremely vital fashion. Consider Canto 1 – 'And then went down to the ship, / Set keel to breakers, . . .' – with the resourceful Odysseus as a mask for the poet in search of his Ithaca. Yet in that very Canto 1 is to be found a clue to the emphasis I place in this account of Pound's poetry and personality.

Disregarding for the moment subtleties concerning cultural 'layering' (Homer out of the Renaissance Andreas Divus, with an Anglo-Saxon rhythm), what is our immediate and relatively naive response to Canto 1? We probably cannot help knowing that it is a retelling of a section of the *Odyssey* in which Odysseus, on the advice of Circe, conjures up shades from the underworld to seek advice from Tiresias about his return to Ithaca. Even if we miss many of the other subtleties that Poundian exegesis can discover for us, we certainly feel the presence of a writer intensely responsive to ritual, to the mystery of death, to the sacred. The delicately pondered archaism of the style, however, should alert us to the fact that here, too, is a writer whose relation to such subject-matter is not quite easy. And the sudden pedantic intrusion of the 'Lie quiet, Divus. I mean, that is Andreas Divus' passage reinforces our premonition of something ironic and distanced in the relation of the poet to the realm of the sacred. Then, with that 'Venerandam' – isolated, incantatory – and with the solemnly spaced phrases invoking Aphrodite that conclude Canto 1, it is as if the writer, by awe-struck insistence, is close to overcoming the irony of distance that we have sensed playing around his response to the mythic and the sacred.

Canto 1's use of Odysseus as 'mask' epitomises an odd effect in the reader's relationship to the past throughout sections of the poem. The poet is not saying, 'I, Pound, poet of the twentieth century, claim for myself the substance of such and such visions and sacramental rituals.' He is saying: 'I, Pound, poet of the twentieth century, am re-enacting these things as if I were Odysseus, or as if I were some remote hypothetical presence, thereby hoping to evoke in you, modern reader, intimations of the sacred and the mythic, but in a tone that erects a subtle barrier – the barrier

of our mutual self-conscious modernity that knows itself
distant from something that is desirable and noble by virtue
of the very style in which those qualities are evoked.' Surely
(leaving aside Canto 1's deliberate Anglo-Saxon stylistic
pastiche) that is something of what we sense in the other
mythical or visionary episodes that occur in the first fifty-
one Cantos. It is as if we were seeing such things through
the eyes of a poet who knows he must re-enact them in a
very ambiguous context. He does so in a manner delicately
aloof, ritualistic and, for all the terse visual power, remote;
with something of that pathos of distance which Panofsky
attributed to the fifteenth-century humanist's view of
classical antiquity in *Renaissance and Renascences.* Around
such scenes and figures in Cantos 1–51 there hovers just the
faint suggestion of that phrase which Pound used in Canto
3: 'As Poggio has remarked.' In other places one could
imagine: 'as Sir James Frazer has remarked . . .' It gives to
the religious feeling of these pre-Pisan Cantos – which is
very intense in spite of the sophistication of tone I have
clumsily tried to convey – a peculiarly poignant authenticity.

Even the strictly historical personages who people the
earlier Cantos, although their being is conveyed with more
obvious immediacy, are continually placed in a context of
stylistic fragmentation and discontinuity which makes *The
Cantos* an elegiac evocation of 'the ruin of history', as
Richard Pevear put it in the moving essay to which reference has already been made. How could one ever fail to see
that the dizzy-making montage, the abrupt discontinuities,
the headlong vituperation, the sharp ironic contrasts of
journalistic argot and commercial corruption with noble
vigour and austere myth, are the expression of desperation
and revolt on the part of a personality inwardly disinte-
grated by the pressures of his acute historicist sensibility?
Not at all the type of 'factive' personality he admired and
wished to be, but a desperately eclectic *déraciné* whose
deepest instincts were those of a visionary and idealist, a
kind of latter-day Shelley with a clean post-Imagist style but
the same passionate awareness of a gulf between vision and
reality:

The integrity of John Adams, the humaneness of
Hapsburg-Lorraine, Kung's vision of order, My Cid
riding up to Burgos, leave the darkness only deeper
after they have flared for a moment and died again.
Donna mi prega illumines just by being beautiful . . .
and inaccessible now that the maid's needle has been
blunted.[8]

Frohock strikes me as right there about Kung
(Confucius), wrong about John Adams. Neither can exactly
be said to 'flare for a moment', since Kung's presence
hovers around all the China section of the poem and John
Adams reminisces remorselessly throughout ten lengthy
Cantos. Yet Confucian China was just the kind of thing to
kindle Pound's imagination. For all their didactic emphasis
on the distinguishing of good emperors (granaries full, low
taxes) from bad emperors (eunuchs in charge, Taozers and
Bhud-foés on the loose), the 'China' Cantos are suffused
with Pound's imaginative response to 'a vision of total
order, celestial, ritualistic, agricultural, aesthetic';[9] and to
the falling away from such order. It is a vision of the kind of
society whose ideal form has haunted the imagination of so
many post–Industrial Revolution intellectuals and artists of
the West; the 'organic' society, where alienation has been
overcome in a regained unity of being. The elegant proces-
sional rhythms of these 'China' Cantos, spiced with calculated modern turns of phrase, align them with the earlier
Cantos by their rendering yet again, though in a different
mode, the elegiac note of Pound's historicism.

In the 'John Adams' Cantos, by contrast, a determined
effort is made to be didactic, constructive, positive. Yet
allowing for some local successes (for example, the account
of Adams' journey through Spain and France in Canto 65),
the total effect is disastrous. The fragmented method of
presentation is intrinsically unsuited to the constructive
purpose, and where pungent vitality was intended there is,
in the main, only aridity. It is like being locked for hours in a
boring committee room full of droning Yankee voices discussing fiscal and constitutional issues; yet just dimly,
through a partition, there is at moments the sound of

distant chamber music – that inimitable personal rhythm which Pound was able to impose on even the most recalcitrant material.

Practice in the type of versified diarising we find at depressing length in the John Adams section of the poem may well, however, have helped Pound to achieve the perfection of the form as it is used in *The Pisan Cantos*. Moreover in the Pisan series, as distinct from the 'Adams' Cantos, formal fragmentation was the perfect medium for the state of mind conveyed. The seemingly artless windings of an interior monologue are full of pointed juxtapositions; memories, personal and historical, are garnered for transmission by some elite of the spirit to a future that is nevertheless barely posited, since we are in a world where 'all time is eternally present' – and redeemable. In *The Pisan Cantos* the poet's own self, having been largely absorbed into mask, pastiche and translation in earlier Cantos, for the first time appears on stage – the histrionic image comes naturally to the pen, and has its odd appropriateness. Whilst there can be no question of the poetry's authenticity of feeling on its own terms, the recurrent use of the Odysseus mask makes for a distancing and universalising effect – 'when the raft broke and the waters went over me' (Canto 80); and such a device helps throw into specially poignant relief the startling directness of certain confessional lines such as:

> I have been hard as youth sixty years
>
> *(Canto 80)*

The Pisan Cantos are at one and the same time intensely personal and intensely stylised; the sections of Cantos 81, 82 and 83 in which a type of religious climax is reached, for example, are decidedly elusive in some of their effects. The poetry is not introspective in the self-gratifying modern manner. Pound conveys poignant memories and observations of the scene around him in the camp with a deftly casual precision, so that we feel the mastery of an extremely artful style in the very rendering of time's tragic dissolutions. The poetry is curiously sharp and detached in its poignancy. The craftsman redeeming the victim:

Butterflies, mint and Lesbia's sparrows,
the voiceless with bumm drum and banners,
               and the ideogram of the guard
                     roosts
   el triste pensier si volge
      ad Ussel. A Ventadour
         va il consire, el tempo rivolge
and at Limoges the young salesman
bowed with such french politeness "No, that is
                   impossible."
I have forgotten which city
But the caverns are less enchanting to the unskilled
                explorer
   than the Urochs as shown on the postals,
we will see those old roads again, question,
             possibly
but nothing appears much less likely,
            Mme Pujol,
and there was a smell of mint under the tent flaps
especially after the rain
     and a white ox on the road toward Pisa
       as if facing the tower,
dark sheep in the drill field and on wet days were
                clouds
in the mountain as if under the guard roosts.
   A lizard upheld me
   the wild birds wd not eat the white bread
             (Canto 74, p. 428)

Of course there is sadness in that; there are consciously elegiac cadences, as, for instance, in Pound's own Italian phrases about memory turning back to Ussel and Ventadour in the Dordogne – sacred places for him. Yet the mind in its terrible isolation seems for the first time able to relax, with all the effortless precision of a master. Loss on such a scale has its balance of gain. Pound's dream of harmony and perfection, the driving-force of his existence, had led him to seek its active realisation on the plane of political action, and to back the wrong side in a hideous war.

When history defeated the poet-reformer, that failed aspiration towards the worldly realisation of goodness, truth and beauty survived 'now in the mind indestructible', whilst civilisation collapsed around him. In the wilds of that mind alone was there to be an Eleusis, a light of the divine, a glimpsed Confucian harmony.

It would be convenient to claim that the story ended on that note: the poet-seer mystically at peace with Confucian immanence. Yet Canto 84, the last of the Pisan series, warns us otherwise. Something tragically flawed, an incompleteness either aggressive or semi-despairing, was to be Pound's lot until the end of his life. It is a moving paradox that the greatness of this poet who set so much store by masks and indirections, and who ostensibly rejected the Romantic role of the poet, should in the end touch us most keenly by the interplay between his work and a disastrous yet exemplary life. The Cantos which followed the Pisan series, *Rock-Drill*, *Thrones* and *Drafts and Fragments*, cannot in my view be separated from the circumstances of the poet's life during and just after his incarceration in St Elizabeth's hospital for the insane. Moreover the almost total silence that descended on the poet thereafter in his last years in Italy, when taken in conjunction with the disillusioned utterances of a few of the final Fragments, endow the totality of his life and work with a coherence and a grandeur that has something of the cathartic effect of great tragedy.

In *Rock-Drill* and *Thrones* two things strike one first. Considerable stretches re-iterate in a disjointed and somewhat nagging fashion the depredations of usurious bankers, the manipulation of credit, and so on. Much lengthier stretches concern themselves with three societies of the past where, in theory and to some extent in practice, just polities had been evolved: tenth-century Byzantium, K'ang-Hsi's China, and (via Coke's seventeenth-century commentaries on the great charters) the English Middle Ages. The reforming and didactic urge is again strong in these Cantos. Such polities must in turn be based on a right grasp of the sacred bases of the cosmic Process with which the poet intimated some kind of personal union at the culmination of *The Pisan Cantos*. We must be struck by the

courageous persistence with which he continued to attempt
a fusion between his intimations of cosmic harmony and the
world of practical politics. 'Only connect', Pound seems to
be saying. . . . Or, as Octavio Paz puts it: 'Poetry is *paideia*.
Those instantaneous visions that rend the shadows of
history as Diana the clouds, are not ideas or things – they
are light. "All things that are are lights." But Pound is not a
contemplative; these lights are acts and they suggest a
course of action.'[10] I disagree with Paz – to me the deepest
notes of the poet are those of a contemplative – but he puts
the opposite point of view extremely well, and Pound
himself would undoubtedly, until a very late stage in his
life, have seen it as being more loyal to his undertaking. Yet
the verdict of aridity and decline which has been passed on
some of these later Cantos strikes me as justified. One can
be stimulated to learn from them, of course; Pound is
seldom less than a teacher. But, as with the 'Adams' Cantos,
fragmentation of form seems inappropriate for the constructive didactic purpose, and, fatal to say, lucid
expositions of their content (for instance by C. F. Terrell, J. J.
Wilhelm or David Gordon) have a tendency to read more
interestingly than many of the sections themselves, as they
lie scattered over the pages of these last Cantos.

Thus much said, should we not remember the circumstances in which Pound had to write his poetry? A man of
extreme though flawed sensitivity confined to a squalid
madhouse; disinclined by temperament to sustain a
mystical quietism in spite of his contemplative intimations;
aware that his own folly, compounding the stroke of fate,
had led him to disaster – who can blame him if he turned
again toward didactic concerns to sustain himself? I am
aware that this may sound condescending. I do not mean it
to be so. There are, of course, remarkable things at this
didactic level. Canto 99, for instance, the re-working of
K'ang Hsi's *Sacred Edict*, is a *tour de force*. More congruent
with Pound's deepest gifts, however, are certain fragments,
brief sections, occasionally whole Cantos of a finely etched
yet ethereal lyricism. The great things in *Rock-Drill*, *Thrones*
and *Last Fragments* are delicately terse pastoral or myth,
punctuated by fragmentary hints of neo-Platonic Light
metaphysics, and touched at moments with a piercing

sadness. The poet's discovery of the Na-Khi material in the course of composing *Thrones* was of deep significance. There, in the unexpected shape of a great botanist's study of an isolated tribe in South West China, was the vision of a kind of Golden Age perfection that could be played off against surrounding darkness and confusion.

The central part played in. the final Cantos by Pound's chance discovery of the customs of this obscure tribe could stand as a symbol of much that we may feel to be typical of his position in twentieth-century culture. An eclectic modern sensibility, exposed to the diversity of the past by a sophisticated historicism, ranges through time fascinated by modes of being very alien to the nature of his own civilisation; and in the course of his time-travelling he is especially drawn to cultures which afford imaginative appeasement to the religious yearnings of a rootless modernity. Thus the terror of history – Mircea Eliade's phrase – is overcome. The Na-Khi religion was a primitive nature-worship, whose essential simplicity should not be overlooked, even though we may find the details of its rites puzzling in Pound's allusive rendering. For, after all, is this not a familiar symptom of modern culture? A post-Romantic sensibility estranged from the numinous by the hostile pressures of Western civilisation seeks assuagement in primitive religiosity; the chaotic self-consciousness of the modern, by some paradoxical feat, cultivates the rituals of permanence in the wilds of its own mind. The most sustained embodiment in *The Cantos* of this circuitous journey to the sacred is to be found in the Pisan series, which tend at their climax towards a quietistic union with cosmic Process – a union rendered in a fashion curiously oblique and stylised. In the years of strain and suffering that followed their composition, the note of yearning for a lost paradise of religious wholeness persisted throughout the didactic emphases of *Rock-Drill* and *Thrones*. The final version of Pound's 'paradise within' was the versifying of the Na-Khi material, which flutes delicate grace-notes to the growing disillusion of *The Cantos'* last fragments.

Such a conclusion seems logical on the hypothesis that Pound was in essence an elegiac poet, drawn to contemplation. Yet something is wrong, something is missing. For instance, the sheer fun of a good deal of *The Cantos* is missing, their brio and their fighting spirit. Thinking back on *Rock-Drill* and *Thrones,* on the details of the nineteenth-century United States Bank War, tenth-century Byzantine trade edicts, and English medieval charters, one realises that the poem needed these things, though perhaps not always in the shape offered in those later instalments of *The Cantos.* They are undoubtedly more confusing and less enlivening than the historical documentation, *obiter dicta* and quirky anecdotes of the early Cantos, yet they serve a similar purpose. They direct the mind outwards to the real world of men, to history, to other cultures. Even though the deepest vein and the ultimate effect of *The Cantos* is elegiac – and I persist in thinking so – Pound's decision to risk the epic omnivorousness, the epic diversity, was a great gain. It saved him from the 'damnosa hereditas' of Symbolist intro-version and preciosity. And what a relief to turn to the ranging allusiveness of *The Cantos* after dieting on so many small lyric utterances of the twentieth century; tough or tender; all navel-gazing. It was curiosity that did the trick. 'Curiosity – advice to the young – curiosity,' affirms the aged poet in Contino's photographic record of his last years in Italy.[11] The elegiac quality of *The Cantos* would be a minor achievement were it not for the tension generated by the passionate, activist side of Pound's nature, as Robert Lowell well saw. Didactic fury was the needful grain of sand that produced the authentic pearl of contemplation.

The quality of that elegiac contemplation, especially in *Last Fragments,* is something very rare in English poetry. There is sadness, a sense of loss. There is disillusion. Yet the disillusion is of too celestial a simplicity to warrant calling it despair. Pound had never been the type of modern writer who is 'cosmically concerned and terrestrially calm', in Conor Cruise O'Brien's deadly phrase.[12] When, therefore, Pasolini requested his support for the world peace move-ment in the USA during his last, silent years in Venice, Pound, part Oedipus at Colonus, part Taoist sage, part unnervingly silent old gentleman, had earned the right to say:

In reply to your question; I think the intentions are good, but I do not think these demonstrations are the right answer. I see things from another angle. As I wrote in a draft for a recent Canto:

> 'When one's friends hate one another
> How can there be peace in the world?'[13]

Pound knew in the end what the tones of his greatest poetry had been implying all along, that he looked in history for a perfection which can only lie beyond history or in the realm of the imagination:

> M'amour m'amour
> what do I love and
> where are you?
> That I lost my centre
> fighting the world.
> The dreams clash
> and are shattered—
> and that I tried to make a paradiso
> terrestre.

He had taken on the Great Beast and been worsted. Perhaps at the end he too had reached the same point as his friend Yeats, who wrote:

> State and Nation are the work of intellect, and when you consider what comes before and after them they are, as Victor Hugo said of something or other, not worth the blade of grass God gives for the nest of the linnet.[14]

1 General Considerations

It is usual to praise *The Pisan Cantos* for their markedly personal quality, and there is obvious truth in the practice. The poet renders the sights and sound of his Pisan prison-camp with sharp, humorous vividness. Evocations of famous friends and of others less famous sustain a tone of reminiscence throughout the series. An unmasked poignancy utters itself in such phrases as 'Oh let an old man rest', 'I have been hard as youth sixty years', even though the poet resorts to French for rendering the ultimate arcanum of his grief: 'Les larmes que j'ai créées m'inondent'. Yet the admittedly very personal *Pisan Cantos* are still patterned in accordance with the prototype of Odyssean-voyage-cum-Dantesque-pilgrimage which is a recurring structural device of the whole poem; and they render as well the universal myths of light and fertility which pervade the rest of *The Cantos*. The other non-Pisan Cantos must in turn be seen not as an impersonal collage of historical pastiche, mythical scene-painting and contemporary satire, but as a personal epic of self-discovery – 'a record of struggle', as the poet wrote in *Guide to Kulchur*[1] – wherein a rootless sensibility of the early twentieth century, sophisticated by the historicism of the nineteenth, embarks on a mental pilgrimage in search of things enduring and redemptive.

In order to render the note of troubled progression which fitly characterises a major work sensitive to the confusions of the modern age, Pound risked carrying to an extreme that freedom from traditional patterns of form which the great progenitors of literary modernism were cultivating in alliance with their fellows in the other arts so as to break free from the conventions which had dominated European culture since the Renaissance. Cubism, Vorticism, Expressionism, for instance, all aimed to do away with representationalism in the visual arts; and music, simultaneously breaking away from the tonal conventions of many centuries, was often invoked by the other arts, at that period of experiment and renewal, as a model of intense and intricate formalisation, independent of mimesis or traditional rhetoric. Hence the swift, achronological transitions, the modelling in terms of theme and echo, the 'subject-rhymes',[2] which are so striking in the structure of *The Cantos* in general and *The Pisan Cantos* in particular, may helpfully be seen against the background of that musicalisation of literary form which was so prominent in the late nineteenth century and persisted in the early-twentieth-century theories of classical modernism. Its appeal can be traced ultimately to Romantic notions of an organic form that is truly expressive of a unique sensibility unfettered by the claims of genre or mimesis; a sensibility whose fluctuations the literary artist must render in a manner intimate, flexible and free.

In Pound's *Gaudier-Brzeska*, for example, the Romantic background of the following passage is striking: 'Our respect is not for the subject-matter, but for the creative power of the artist; for that which he is capable of adding to his subject from himself; or, in fact, his capability to dispense with external subjects altogether, to create from himself or from elements.' So much for the expressionist basis of the outlook. Later in the same work Pound characterises the form that should emerge by quoting approvingly from Whistler and then commenting himself: ' "The artist is born to pick and choose, and *group with science*, these elements, that the result may be beautiful – as the musician gathers his notes and forms his chords." One uses form as a musician uses sound. One does not imitate the wood-dove, or at least one does not confine oneself to the imitation of wood-doves, one combines and arranges one's sound or one's form into Bach fugues or into arrange-

ments of colour, or into "planes in relation".' And in
another part of the same work Pound writes: 'We return
again and again to Pater's "all arts approach the conditions
of music" . . . I am aware that most people cannot feel form
"musically". That they get no joy, no thrill from an arrange-
ment of planes. That they have no sense of form.'[3]

I have quoted from *Gaudier-Brzeska* at some length in
order to show the persistence in a great classical modernist
like Pound of a post-Romantic and Symbolist attachment to
music as a model for literary form. In those very quotations,
however, there were visual analogies as well, although
admittedly of a Cubist kind – 'planes in relation'. And we
also do well to remember that Pound was a leading pro-
ponent of Imagism. In spite of the visual connotations of the
word, however, Pound's Imagism was never a narrow
visualist doctrine, as Herbert Schneidau has shown; rather
it was aimed at maximum verbal condensation for the
releasing of formal energy. Yet Schneidau rightly reminds
us too of the 'etched quality' in all Pound's best work,[4] and
any stress on musical analogies that might make Pound
seem like a misty Debussyite Impressionist is to be avoided.
I allude to music merely because this least obviously
mimetic of the arts was such a useful analogy for a literary
artist bent on breaking with conventions of rhetorical
progression and logical development so as to render more
authentically the elements which his individual creative
force was attracting into new configurations of formal
energy – I speak of Pound's 'Vortex'. This is a concept
which *The Pisan Cantos* exemplify more fully perhaps than
any other group of Cantos, and which is beautifully touched
on in a closing line of Canto 74: 'so light is the urging, so
ordered the dark petals of iron'. A line that in turn is
clarified by a passage from *Guide to Kulchur* which clearly
meant much to Pound:

> The *forma*, the immortal *concetto*, the concept, the
> dynamic form which is like the rose pattern driven into
> the dead iron-filings by the magnet, not by material
> contact with the magnet itself, but separate from the
> magnet. Cut off by the layer of glass, the dust and

filings rise and spring into order. Thus the *forma,* the concept rises from death.

> The bust outlasts the throne
> The coin Tiberius.[5]

That passage, in spite of its elegant classicising gesture in the final quotation, should again alert us to the Romantic origins of Pound's attitude to poetic structure, which is something that the poem generates of itself if the poetic response to the elements of experience is sufficiently intense to attract them into a 'dynamic' form. There is no predetermined mould for experience, but rather a continuous charge of psychic energy which activates the most surprisingly disparate elements. Hence the exciting tentativeness of *The Cantos*: they show us light amidst a variety of shifting perspectives; they make the effect of something turning inward upon itself by virtue of internal echoes; yet they are continuously receptive to new experience by virtue of their open form. They take in an immense range of material, indeed their sheer factuality can be daunting at times; yet they contrive in an odd fashion to be intensely personal and self-regarding as well. It is usual to stress that Pound's imagist-ideographic method makes his poem essentially different from the autotelic structures of the Symbolist imagination where words, like notes in music, create a non-mimetic world of pure feeling. And indeed it is true that Pound's gaze is directed outwards, the flexible form of *The Cantos* being receptive of ever-new ranges of material acquired in the course of a lifetime. The poet carves at the block of the real so as to elicit a shape that is potentially there – 'the stone knows the form' – as Donald Davie has always stressed. *The Cantos* are full of things really said, deeds really done, past systems of value re-presented. Yet there is still something ambiguous about the factual, objective nature of *The Cantos,* and I think this is due to the poem's having largely abandoned linear construction, narrative mimesis, and to its depending for coherence on internal echoes and subject-rhymes. This makes it curiously self-regarding and self-sufficient, like a Symbolist work; and we could well feel, at times, that the deepest reality with which we make contact in *The Cantos* is one quicksilver modern self. At any rate that is why we may be tempted to see *The Pisan Cantos* as the fulfilment of the poet's truest gift, since in them an essentially lyric and subjective impulse is no longer straining to energise intractable historical and didactic material along some timeless continuum, but absorbs time and history into the soliloquising intensity of its own dream.

Pound's epic attempt, though it contains some of the familiar components of myth, sacred legend and history that are the common property of the European consciousness – the *Odyssey*, the *Divine Comedy* – utilises as well the heterogeneous learning and interests of an isolated eclectic mind of the twentieth century. Hence the attempt on Pound's own terms to establish archetypal patterns of human existence, though moving and impressive, must in the nature of the case seem an arbitrary invention rather than the deeper revelation of hallowed truths and events achieved by the traditional epic in more cohesive cultures.[6] And though the narrative structure of traditional epic is not necessarily that of straightforward temporal progression, the effect is certainly not comparable to the echoes and improvisations of *The Cantos*.

The contrast with Dante is instructive. For all the importance of Dante as an influence on *The Cantos*, Pound's order is not one of single steady ascent, emblematic of an ordered universe and sublime assurance. Though there are discernibly more 'Paradiso' concerns from the Pisan series onwards, to see the work as articulated in too coherent an Inferno–Purgatory–Paradise sequence has never struck me as convincing. There are too many variations and subtleties of layering. Pound had, as he put it, no 'Aquinas-map';[7] hence his form aims to catch the difficult, sporadic nature of Order and Light. Those qualities are ontologically real for Pound, I feel sure; man dwells in a cosmos that is not beholden to him alone. 'Pull down thy vanity, it is not man / Made courage, or made order, or made grace, / Pull down thy vanity, I say pull down. / Learn of the green world what can be thy place / In scaled invention or true artistry.' Remarkable in so seemingly rootless and eclectic a sensibility, Pound's religious sense is fundamental to any understanding of him – a sense of the numinous and the sacred being the very heart of *The Cantos*. This sense is appropriately mirrored, however, in the formal fragmentation and stylistic obliqueness of his work, so as to render a very modern self in all its limitations and its greatness; and though Pound may have had his fierce certitudes and achieved clarities, they were reached and sustained in a context very different from the Dantescan universe. That he knew there was a risk of solipsism in attempting to give public validity to the religious intimations of an isolated modern sensibility can be seen from a fragment of *Guide to Kulchur*:

> And a modern Eleusis being possible in the wilds of a man's mind only?[8]

Such a sceptical utterance, surprising in the 1930s, when Pound was at his most crusading, catches in memorable fashion what we may well feel to be the central drama of *The Cantos*. Pound's imagination craved the rituals of permanence, symbolised by Eleusis, yet he could best render that craving in a manner which seemed to hint at how distant such an ideal of permanence must be for a modern mind. 'The wilds of a man's mind' is a phrase rather similar in implication to that other phrase where Pound describes *The Cantos* as 'a record of struggle'. In the course of subsequent chapters I shall be emphasising this note of struggle; the oblique fragmented nature of Pound's wrestling with religious mystery in *The Pisan Cantos*. It will, however, be convenient to summarise first some of the principal ideological components of his outlook, with a stress on *The Pisan Cantos*, but bearing in mind as well their presence in *The Cantos* as a whole.

The cosmic harmony with which Pound's spirit aspires to blend by acts of creative memory under the influence of Aphrodite and Artemis – the role of mythology will be touched on later – is a harmony composed of diverse elements. These elements have all appeared at various stages of earlier Cantos, and will appear again in subsequent ones, but in the Pisan series they attain a closer synthesis. From Confucianism, Eleusinian mystery-cults, Greek mythology and neo-Platonic Light metaphysics, this most determined of modern literary eclectics constructed a religious outlook of disconcerting individuality. Let us begin with a quotation from Pound's translation of *Chung Yung – The Unwobbling Pivot* – the most metaphysical of the classic books of Confucianism, with a passage where the sage defines the nature of that ultimate reality which Pound calls Process:

1.
   Hence the highest grade of this clarifying activity has no limit, it neither stops nor stays.

2.
   Not coming to a stop, it endures; continuing durable, it arrives at the minima (the seeds whence movement springs).

3.
   From these hidden seeds it moves forth slowly but goes far and with slow but continuing motion it penetrates the solid, penetrating the solid it comes to shine forth on high.

4.
   With this penetration of the solid it has effects upon things, with this shining from on high, that is with its clarity of comprehension, now here, now yonder, it stands in the emptiness above with the sun, seeing and judging, interminable in space and in time, searching, enduring, and therewith it perfects even external things.

5.
   In penetrating the solid it is companion to the brotherly earth (offers the cup of mature wine to the earth) standing on high with the light of the intellect it is companion of heaven persisting in the vast, and in the vast of time, without limit set to it.

6.

Being thus in its nature; unseen it causes harmony; unmoving it transforms; unmoved it perfects.

7.

The celestial and earthly process can be defined in a single phrase; its actions and its creations have no duality. (The arrow has not two points).[9]

Notable in that passage is the stress on harmony. The workings of earth and heaven, body and mind, are subsumed under a single organic process which has 'no duality'. Sin, tension, polarity, are quite absent from the vision of the whole to which this poet's imagination responds; and in the Confucian philosophy the personal, social and political spheres of existence are seen as contributory harmonies within one larger cosmic harmony. If 'world-views' on the grand scale are held to be attitudes towards existence, rather than factual truths about existence, one may well feel that an aesthetic temperament would find this world-view especially pleasing. It was the sense of a harmonious permanence underlying change that most impressed Pound when he contemplated the history of China; a millennial stability due to good emperors who ordered the individual in a right relationship to the state, and maintained both state and individual in a right relationship to the generative powers of Nature and hence to the religious wholeness of universal Process.

Pound's 'China' Cantos persistently illustrate such a view, as does one typical allusion in *The Pisan Cantos:*

Shun's will and
King Wan's will

were as the two halves of a seal

(Canto 77, p. 467)

Pound explains in his Mencius essay[10] that these two emperors, divided by a thousand years in time – that is the point – participated in one 'paideuma', or civilised tradition based on a correct awareness of organic Process. They were sustainers of the Good Society, architects of the Just City: a theme that Pound expands in the dauntingly philological Byzantium of his *Thrones* (Cantos 96–109) and in his re-working of Coke's seventeenth-century commentaries on the great English medieval charters. Herodotus' Deioces, builder of Ecbatan, another holy city of the ancient world, plays the same role at the opening of *The Pisan Cantos* –

> To build the city of Dioce whose terraces are the colour
> of stars

– as does Mussolini, by association with Deioces, in the same opening passage. Later in the series Mussolini's presence is felt in lines like these:

> 'not a right but a duty'
> those words still stand uncancelled,
> 'Presente!'
> and merrda for the monopolists
> the bastardly lot of 'em
> Put down the slave trade, made the desert to yield
> and menaced the loan swine
>
> *(Canto 78, p. 479)*

The attitude of responsible government, attributed in those lines to Mussolini, on account of his attempt to break the power of usurious bankers who pervert the bounty of the natural order for private gain, is what won for him his pride of place at the opening of *The Pisan Cantos*. We must put out of mind the Mussolini who was the butt of English and American wartime propagandists and remember that for Pound he was a ruler whose Confucian intentions were frustrated and betrayed in practice:

> The enormous tragedy of the dream in the peasant's
> bent shoulders
> Manes! Manes was tanned and stuffed,
> Thus Ben and la Clara *a Milano*
> by the heels at Milano

That maggots shd/ eat the dead bullock
DIGONOS, Δίγονος, but the twice crucified
where in history will you find it?
(Canto 74, p. 425)

This evocation of Mussolini's murder, followed by the defilement ('twice crucified') at Milan of his own body and that of his mistress, Clara Petacci, is flanked with references to the religious prophet Manes, the crucified victim of a blinded populace; to a dead bullock, with its probable over-tones of sacrificial victim;[11] and to the god Dionysos by way of one of his epithets 'Δίγονος', 'twice-born'. Dionysos has figured throughout *The Cantos* as a symbol of all 'the mysteries and uncontrollable tides that ebb and flow in the life of nature'.[12] Consequently Mussolini, who tried to be a just ruler, is associated through the Dionysos reference with the sacred energies of the cosmos, especially in their aspect of fertility and rebirth. Moreover Dionysos, thus promi-nently evoked at the beginning of the Pisan series, played some part in the Eleusinian mysteries, which in turn were associated by Pound in the opening Canto (52) of the Chinese series with that right relationship to the order of the cosmos which Confucian China attained.

This seems the moment to turn to the Eleusinian element in Pound's religious outlook, an element already prominent in Cantos 39 and 47, but still more dominant in *The Pisan Cantos*. In the words of Miyake, 'the Eleusinian rites express the two rudimentary notions in the cosmos, the human aspiration to return to heaven and heaven's blessing the earth with fertility'.[13] When Pound in the famous 'Usura' Canto (45) wrote of the post-medieval world's substituting 'whores for Eleusis' it was because the resources of the natural world, symbolised by corn – Demeter was an Eleusinian corn-deity – were part of a sacred totality; while usury was the symptom of a desecration of those resources for private gain. All the gritty economics that occur in *The Cantos,* as well as their savage exemplification of economic corruption, look different when seen in the light of Pound's religious awe at the generative energies of the cosmos. The Orage circle which aroused his concern with economic and political matters, when *The Cantos* were in their early stages, was itself pervaded by religious theories of a heterodox type. Orage and the *New Age* circle espoused a Guild Socialism which, opposed to both Capitalism and Communism and akin to the Fascist doctrine of the corporate state, was permeated by the *Illuminé* outlook. 'Orage', writes James Webb, 'was a prominent theosophist . . . very many of the circle around Orage were later to vow allegiance to one or another guru . . . the movement was idealistic, concerned with the functional and organic view of life, and could be justly called "reactionary" – in the sense that it derived its inspiration from an idealised historical example, rather than an equally idealised vision of a future society.'[14] C. H. Douglas's Social Credit movement, with which Pound is more commonly identified, also emerged from the *New Age* circle, and Douglas's more technical economic theories concerning the crucially deleterious role of cost-accounting in the capitalist system were rooted in Guild ideas about the just price and the horrors of usury. Moreover, as Webb shows, there was even an admixture of religious Illuminism and occult mysticism in the Social Credit movement itself.

Political and economic theorising was, then, part of a total vision of life, individualistic and heterodox in its religious basis, with roots in the Gnostic and Illuminist underground tradition of European civilisation. And Pound's admiration for a guru-type figure like Allen Upward makes a special kind of sense in this context. When we add that these economic theorists and *Illuminés* often had Fascist and anti-Semitic leanings, it is obvious that the various strands brought together in chapter II of Webb's book are of profound importance for understanding Pound's development. The poet's belief that the modern world was in the thrall of Usury is directly linked to his Illuminist fascination with the mysteries of Eleusis. Since the fertility ritual at Eleusis is associated with the myth of Demeter and Persephone, or Kore, they are prominently invoked at key points of *The Pisan Cantos* to indicate a right relationship to the sacred energies of Nature on the part of the Greek culture which gave them birth. Eleusis was also always favourably contrasted by Pound with the asceticism and consequent dualism introduced into European culture by medieval Christianity; Usura and asceticism being twin perversions of goods at once natural and sacred. From this derive, I think, the Eleusinian overtones in Canto 82 where the poet's reconciliation to the prospect of death is a celebration of the mysteries of the earth to which he sees himself in the erotic relationship of 'connubium terrae', 'spouse of the earth'. Also woven into the passage are references to the new life that will spring from the earth to which the body will be joined at death. More patently Eleusinian, with its flanking references to Persephone, is the conclusion of the marvellous passage in Canto 83 where a new-born wasp, observed by Pound from his rough tent in the Pisan prison-camp, exemplifies, on a tiny scale, the enormous chthonic powers of generation; whilst its disappearance, through the green grass into the earth, is seen as an emblem of that intercourse between the realms of the living and the dead which promises the renewal and rebirth we associate with Persephone's part in the Eleusinian rite. The passage is capped by a reference to the resurrected Christ as a sun-god. Pound, true to his syncretising post-Frazerian interest in the universal archetypes of religious belief, sees Christ's story as one more myth illustrating the perpetual renewal of the sacred process of life:

> The infant has descended,
>   from mud on the tent roof to Tellus,
>   like to like colour he goes amid grass-blades
>   greeting them that dwell under XTHONOS
>   ΧΘΟΝΟΣ
> ΟΙ ΧΘΟΝΙΟΙ;   to carry our news
>   εἰς χθονιους   to them that dwell under the
>   earth
> begotten of air, that shall sing in the bower
>   of Kore,   Περσεφόνεια
> and have speech with Tiresias, Thebae
>   Cristo Re, Dio Sole
>   *(Canto 83, p. 533)*

Thus far I have been stressing the fertility aspects of Eleusis, and the analogy which Pound saw between Eleusis and the piety of Confucian emperors who tended their state with an awareness of its dependence on a sacred Process. The sentence of Miyake quoted earlier stressed also the importance of 'the human aspiration to return to heaven' in the Eleusinian context. The hierophant at Eleusis, as well as participating in a fertility ritual, was the recipient of an illumination, an experience of Light. Miyake also states, in the course of her impressive work, that 'one can believe Pound convinced himself that the Eleusinian mystery was developed into Christian mysticism',[15] and she points out the similarity between the stages of the ritual undergone by the hierophant at Eleusis and the progress of the soul in Christian mysticism. If Miyake's link is justified, one can see how attractive it must have been for Pound to derive what was valid for him in Christian mysticism from a fertility ritual which stressed the harmonious unity of man and nature. Thus the single Confucian Process, in which there is 'no duality', could be seen under the aspect of generation in Eleusinian fertility ritual, and under the aspect of light in Christian or non-Christian neo-Platonic mysticism.

Pound's belief that 'a light from Eleusis persisted throughout the middle ages and set beauty in the song of Provence and Italy'[16] also belongs to the cluster of ideas we are considering, since for him that beauty was linked with the persistence of pagan mysteries in courtly love; and courtly love in turn was linked with neo-Platonic light metaphysics. A concentrate of all these beliefs is to be seen in Pound's terminological note on the MING ideogram at the beginning of his translation of Confucius' *Ta Hio* (*The Great Digest*). There he aligns Confucian light and Christian neo-Platonic light, the latter exemplified by John Scotus Erigena and Robert Grosseteste. The thirteenth-century Italian love-poet Cavalcanti appears in the note as well, since Pound in part linked him with neo-Platonic light metaphysics, and gave him a prominent place in *The Cantos* by translating his 'Donna mi priegha' *canzone* as Canto 36:

明   The sun and moon, the total light process, the radiation, reception and reflection of light; hence, the intelligence. Bright, brightness, shining. Refer to Scotus Erigena, Grosseteste and the notes on light in my *Cavalcanti*.

Scotus Erigena, a ninth-century Christian neo-Platonist particularly valued by Pound because he was condemned by a later council of the church for his unorthodox derivation of authority from right reason, was responsible for an utterance that came to mean a great deal to the poet: 'Omnia quae sunt, lumina sunt' ('All things that are, are lights').[17] It is echoed in the following passage of Canto 74, near the beginning of the Pisan series, a passage whose implications for Pound's work it is important to stress. We should note that another Confucian light ideogram (HSIEN) is juxtaposed to a fragment of that talismanic sentence of Scotus Erigena:

> Linus, Cletus, Clement
> > whose prayers,
> the great scarab is bowed at the altar
> the green light gleams in his shell
> plowed in the sacred field and unwound the silk
> > worms early
> > in tensile
> in the light of light is the *virtù*
> > "sunt lumina" said Erigena Scotus
> > as of Shun on Mt Taishan
> and in the hall of the forebears
> > as from the beginning of
> > wonders
> the paraclete that was present in Yao, the precision
> in Shun the compassionate
> in Yu the guider of waters

> > > *(Canto 74, pp. 428–9)*

The central pairing of Confucius and Erigena in the above passage is surrounded by a reference to early Catholic saints invoked in ritual; by an Egyptian prayer ritual; by a Chinese fertility ritual (which might in turn make one think of Eleusinian parallels); by a mention of Mount Taishan, the holy mountain of Chinese religion, whose fancied equivalent, visible from the camp at Pisa, was a constant solace to the poet; and by certain ideal Chinese emperors praised by Confucius, one of whom is referred to as 'Paraclete'. There could not be a better passage to exemplify the syncretism of this poet. Yet is syncretism really the apt word? There is little systematic attempt in Pound to harmonise theoretically the various religious modes that take possession of his imagination. Rather, each is a mode imaginatively valid in the terms of its own culture for rendering an ineffable reality, though certain modes, in particular the neo-Platonised Confucian light process, offer the poet his most comprehensive intimation.

Why does Pound dwell so persistently on light in his religious symbolism all through *The Cantos*, from the famous passage at the end of the second 'Hell' Canto (15) where Plotinus – Pound had not at that stage discovered Erigena – guides the poet in his ascent from the infernal depths of usurious infertility into the light, to the wonderful passages on light that are scattered in *Rock-Drill*, *Thrones* and other closing Cantos? It is helpful to remember that from the time when Pound set out to purge English poetry of its post-Romantic afflatus he valued above all things sharpness of outline and concision of phrasing; even in the most exalted flights of *The Cantos* that 'etched quality' is preserved. Not only in art but in his study of politics and economics, Pound preferred an assemblage of luminous details forming an 'ideogrammic' unity to ordinary logic or compendious abstraction. On these grounds even the superficially confusing fragmentation of *The Pisan Cantos* is a necessary consequence of Pound's attachment to light, since the interaction of details, individually sharp and luminous, is intended to form a whole whose clarity has not been distorted by formalism of a too easy kind.[18]

Pound's temperament combined two factors not often found together at such a level of intensity: a markedly twentieth-century response to the sheer flux of experience, reflected in his attraction to the idea of metamorphosis and in the associative aspects of *The Cantos* – a factor which led Yvor Winters to condemn Pound, and Wyndham Lewis to qualify his praise; counterbalanced by an equally marked search for the permanent, the archetypal, the orderly beauty of form, in politics and art, which culminated in his attraction to a metaphysic of light as revealer of form. In the opening of the whole poem, Aphrodite, at the climax of the first Canto, rises from the waves; apt emblem of form educed from the flux, and of the redemptive goal Odysseus-Pound would have to seek on his journey (periplum) through time and history. In *The Pisan Cantos,* the reformer having been defeated by events, the artist is left alone amidst the 'wreckage of Europe' to struggle towards union with cosmic light; to struggle through acts of contemplation and creative memory that must do justice to the discontinuity of the flux as well as to the order and light intermittently perceived. Aphrodite, fittingly, still hovers over the Pisan series as one of the deities by whom this light is transfused. It is thus not surprising that in the wider sphere of ontology, Pound, from among the small group of images traditionally used to convey the nature of ultimate reality, should have been attracted to light. I know no better account of the attraction of light for religious thought than this passage from Edwyn Bevan's Gifford Lectures, *Symbolism and Belief*:

> The other property of light which has made it serve for a symbol is the way in which a luminous body apparently sends forth, without any force coming into play or any loss being suffered, emanations of its substance, which, to whatever distance they may reach, remain always one with the luminous body, derivative from it not by a momentary event accomplished and done, but by a mode of derivation continuous and always the same. The religious application of this property of light would naturally not be suggested till the idea had come up of derivative Divine beings emanating from God or begotten by God, or proceeding from God, who had an existence of their own and yet remained one with God. Such an idea of Beings in one way identical with God and in another way distinct from God might obviously seem to involve a contradiction, and when men cast about for some figure which might make the apparent contradiction intelligible, the analogy of a luminous body and the ray proceeding from it almost immediately presented itself.[19]

It will be evident from this passage that any thinker prone

to stressing the continuum of light as a symbol for the pervasiveness of the divine may tend towards pantheism. That was one reason for orthodox theological mistrust of Erigena; by contrast it is what Pound, with his Confucian stress on immanence and 'non-duality', particularly valued. Since he believed, moreover, that the best religious insights of Greek mythology were in harmony with this non-dualistic religious position, it is not surprising to find Pound continuing in *The Pisan Cantos* to make effective use of the personages of Greek mythology in order to express his intimations of the sacred. At an earlier stage of *The Cantos* he was inclined to stress the pre-eminence that Ovid's *Metamorphoses* held for him as a holy book, since 'what the tales of the gods show forth is the fertilisation of the natural by the supernatural, the making of the two worlds into one' as well as 'the mystery of the presence of a permanent and unchanging principle throughout all the seeming flux of this universe, in which things come into existence, grow, reproduce, age, and die'.[20] And just as a Renaissance neo-Platonist could offer traditional stories of the gods and goddesses as aspects of the divine Mind, or 'Nous',[21] so Pound felt free to use them as figures of special imaginative potency for a man of Mediterranean culture, within the broader context of what, by the time he wrote *The Pisan Cantos,* we may well label a neo-Platonised Confucianism, where Eleusis also figured as valid myth. Aphrodite, the original symbol of divine beauty, who emerged at the end of the very first Canto, continues to play a part; in the Pisan series she seems to merge with Artemis, the moon-goddess, and a complex symbolism of moon and sun can be traced throughout *The Pisan Cantos*, as Daniel Pearlman has shown in his discussion of the 'culminating vision' in Cantos 81 and 83:

> Fusion of sun and moon in the *Ming* ideogram is, as a matter of fact, the end or goal of the whole symbolic process involving the moon goddesses, with Aphrodite at their head, as intercessors between the poet and the sun. The moon, as reflector of the sun's light and as the gentle, feminine counterpart of Helios, has become the half-way point at which the poet's

subjectivity is finally merged with the objective
process. Throughout *The Pisan Cantos*, both the
successful invocation of Aphrodite and the whole
course of mystic fusion occur before sunrise, that is,
before the distinctions between subject and object are
sharply marked by the light of day, which revives the
painful sights and sounds of the camp enclosure. The
poet never revels in the full light of the sun until after
the intercessor, like the moon nymph of Hagoromo,
reveals her most guarded secrets to her devoted priest
and grants him the culminating vision. Full of the
certitude of his revelation, the poem can then become
reconciled with the sun, which is the light of *reason* in
the cosmic symbology of these cantos.[22]

That passage from Pearlman's impressive and illumi-
nating book draws together complicated symbolic threads
into a magisterial synthesis of the meaning of *The Pisan
Cantos*. Yet its satisfying air of conclusiveness surely misses
something of the improvisatory and oblique quality of the
work. Much criticism is prone to auto-intoxication of the
categories, and Pound's *Cantos*, by their elusive ebb and
flow, positively provoke the critic into teasing out
expository coherence. My own abstracting of religious and
philosophical 'themes' in the course of this chapter has itself
been an example of the same tendency – indeed, a far more
dangerous procedure than anything that can be attributed
to Pearlman. Such neutral thematic exposition may be of
some use in establishing the poet's universe of values, but,
as Earl Wasserman reminds us, 'the final goal of a critical
reading is not to discover the universe in which the work
functions but the way in which it functions in that universe'.

The mode of existence of *The Pisan Cantos* is fragmented,
oblique, spiralling. Hence even to refer to 'The Pattern of
the Pisan Cantos', as Forrest Read does in the title of his
justly famous and influential article, risks a wrong impression rather similar in kind to the brisk finality of Pearlman's
paragraph. 'Pattern' suggests that the critic is viewing
things from on high, whence the essential contours of the
terrain can be plainly mapped. Might not a word like
'labyrinth' catch the intrinsic quality of the work a little

better? In a labyrinth one follows one's nose, backs hunches, finds clues – and feels by the end that if one has stayed the course and emerged at the centre it is as much from luck as from good judgment! Of course the labyrinth analogy is imperfect, and ultimately obfuscatory. It will be best to eschew theory and move directly to examine a passage in some detail, even at the risk of the tedium which a line-by-line commentary can so easily cause; it will at any rate be a way of getting to know how Pound's mind works, in a section that establishes the personal drama of the Pisan series as well as any other. It is not a passage that shows his powers at their height; for that we must await discussion of Cantos 81, 82 and 83. But it gives a good measure of his obsessive concerns and will allow us, as well, to draw out an aspect of *The Cantos* which is of fundamental importance.

2 The Heroic Paradigm

By the square elm of Ida
  40 geese are assembled
(little sister who could dance on a sax-pence)
      to arrange a pax mundi
            Sobr' un zecchin'!   5
Cassandra, your eyes are like tigers,
    with no word written in them
You also have I carried to nowhere
        to an ill house and there is
              no end to the journey.   10
              The chess board too lucid
the squares are too even . . . theatre of war . . .
'theatre' is good. There are those who did not want
    it to come to an end

and those negroes by the clothes-line are
                    extraordinarily like the   15
          figures del Cossa
Their green does not swear at the landscape
2 months' life in 4 colours
      ter flebiliter: Ityn
to close the temple of Janus bifronte   20
      the two-faced bastard
'and the economic war has begun'
        Napoleon wath a goodth man, it took uth
        20 yearth to crwuth him

it will not take uth 20 years to crwuth Mussolini'   25
    as was remarked in via Balbo by the Imperial
                            Chemicals
its brother.
    Firms failed as far off as Avignon . . .
. . . my red leather note-book
                    pax Medicea   30
  by his own talk in Naples, Lorenzo
    who left lyrics inoltre
    that men sing to this day
'alla terra abbandonata'
              followed him Metastasio;   35
'alla' non 'della' in il Programma di Verona
  the old hand as stylist still holding its cunning
and the water flowing away from that side of the lake
is silent as never at Sirmio
      under the arches   40
Foresteria, Salò, Gardone
    to dream the Republic. San Sepolchro
    the four bishops in metal
lapped by the flame, amid ruin, la fede—
    reliquaries seen on the altar.   45
'Someone to take the blame if we slip up on it'
Goedel's sleek head in the midst of it,
    the man out of Naxos past Fara Sabina
'if you will stay for the night'
'it is true there is only one room for the lot of us'   50
'money is nothing'
'no, there is nothing to pay for that bread'
            'nor for the minestra'
'Nothing left here but women'
      'Have lugged it this far, will keep it'
            (il zaino)   55
    No, they will do nothing to you.
'Who *says* he is an American'
    a still form on the branda, Bologna
'Gruss Gott', 'Der Herr!' 'Tatile ist gekommen!'
    Slow lift of long banners   60
      Roma profugens Sabinorum in terras
and belt the citye quahr of nobil fame
  the lateyn peopil taken has their name

bringing his gods into Latium
                    saving the bricabrac   65
'Ere he his goddis brocht in Latio'
              'each one in the name'
in whom are the voices, keeping hand on the reins
Gaudier's word not blacked out
                    nor old Hulme's, nor Wyndham's,
Mana aboda.   71
                              (Canto 78, pp. 477–9)

That opening section of Canto 78 conveys Pound's attitude
to the war which led to his being imprisoned near Pisa, and
also gives an impression of his situation during the last
months of the war. To strike such a biographical note fits
well with what makes for the unity of *The Pisan Cantos* at one
simple level: the poet in a camp near Pisa, his impressions of
it, and of what led up to it. This opening section of Canto 78
is also a good example of how Pound's mind continually
fuses the situation of himself and others in the present with
analogous persons or situations in the past, thus achieving a
kind of timeless universality whose ambiguous effect I shall
draw out at the end of this chapter.

The passage from Canto 78 we are now to examine is
pervaded by impressions of flight, betrayal and desecration:
the flux in its most destructive aspect. Yet, typical of the
Pisan series to a greater or lesser extent, counterpointed by
elusive images of things more constant and serene.

'Counterpoint' is a term which should be applied with
caution to literature, yet at the very opening of Canto 78,
lines 1–5, there is a clear example of Pound's attempting to
approximate it. Let us separate one of the two 'themes',
discuss it in isolation, and then see how it counterpoints the
other.

       (little sister who could dance on a sax-pence)
....
                    Sobr' un zecchin'!

'Little sister' is 'sorella la luna' ('my sister the moon'),
who appeared on the first page of *The Pisan Cantos* as a
manifestation of that cosmic Process which is the perma-

nent setting of the transient phenomena of history; and both Artemis, the moon, and the 'Venus' star recur in *The Pisan Cantos* as settings that release in the poet his stream of creative memory. More directly bearing on this opening passage, however, is a passage at the very end of the preceding Canto 77, where the moon was also imaged as dancing on a coin ('che ballava sobr' un zecchin' '), and the context shows that it is an image not only of vital grace but of clarity of focus as well. (Perhaps it was the simple literal event of seeing moonlight glimmering on a coin that gave Pound his image, though a literary source may of course be concealed there.) Precision of focus as well as vital grace, which is what the moon image renders at the beginning of Canto 78 also, is close to the concept of 'sinceritas', which occurs early in Canto 74 and is Pound's version of the Confucian ideogram for the precise definition of words.[1] Pound dissected that ideogram into 'the sun's lance coming to rest on the precise spot' – an image close to that of a shaft of moonlight on a coin. From all this we see that the latter image, having been associated with an ideogram of precise focus and 'sinceritas', contains all Pound's implied trust in Confucian wisdom.

Thus much for the associations of clarity and precision rendered in one of the pair of themes in that little *fugato* opening of Canto 78. What of the other?

> By the square elm of Ida
> 40 geese are assembled
> ....
> to arrange a pax mundi

Sarcastic contempt is patent in '40 geese'. Geese, squabbling, raucous birds, are no fit contrivers of a 'pax mundi'. Furthermore, they are doing it 'by the square elm of Ida' – that is, Mount Ida, a sacred place of the ancient world. This note of desecration is strengthened in a way relevant to what follows by the reference in the Annotated Index to Mount Ida as 'the scene of the marriage between Anchises and Aphrodite'.[2] Aphrodite, together with Artemis and Persephone, is a presiding deity in *The Pisan Cantos,* and a hint at her presence along with that of the moon, Artemis, sounds the note of sacred presences and their desecration. Moreover the offspring of Aphrodite and Anchises was Aeneas, who figures later in our passage as founder of the Roman Empire and as a pilgrim-hero figure analogous to Mussolini and to the poet himself; he is a variant of the Odysseus persona. I shall, however, reserve discussion of Aeneas until this passage occurs, at lines 60–7.

Thus far, we have an opening passage which contrasts vital grace, precision and clarity with a contemptuous image of desecration – geese arranging a 'pax mundi' on Mount Ida. The 'pax mundi' is the peace conference of 1945 among the Allied victors of World War II. The principal figures at this gathering were an American President who had succeeded to the policies of the hated Roosevelt, betrayer of the American Constitution; Stalin, the shrewd representative of a system totally misguided; and Churchill, the whisky-sodden, warmongering tool of usurious capitalists. So, at any rate, they appeared to Pound; and it certainly reminds us how alien his view of the Second World War and its outcome was from the *idée reçue* of much of the Western world. A telling biographical instance of this occurs in Charles Olson's account of an interview with Pound, just after the war, in St Elizabeth's:

> He told Connie and me that one of the (unpublished) cantos contains the tale of a girl of Rimini who had been raped and who leads a company of Canadians who had asked to be directed to —— across a minefield instead. She also was blown up, both legs off. But it enabled two German prisoners to escape. The payoff came when Pound says 'She was one of the resistance'. . . . he makes no heroine of her. . . . He told it as a tale of war. But he also told it as a deed of one on his side.[3]

We should not be surprised at that – Olson assures us he wasn't – and it could even induce a chastening sense of perspective. More typical of Pound's attitude to the war, however, and undoubtedly less jarring, is the ending of Canto 76:

> po'eri di'aoli
> po'eri di'aoli sent to the slaughter
>   Knecht gegen Knecht
>   to the sound of the bumm drum, to eat remnants
>   for a usurer's holiday to change the
> price of a currency
>
> *(Canto 76, pp. 462–3)*

The 'po'eri di'aoli' echo the 'poor devils out there in the cold at Sorano' of the 'Malatesta' Cantos: simple soldiers on both sides who are the eternal victims, throughout history, of unscrupulous men in high places. For Pound the Second World War was no struggle between a lily-white Democracy and a diabolic Fascism, but one terrible episode in the perennial warfare waged against those who try – like Mussolini – to protect nature and humanity from the depredations of usurious capitalists and their political tools. No wonder that in Canto 78 Pound turns from his sarcastic picture of the 1945 peace conference to evoke Cassandra, whose very name suggests doom and prophecies un-heeded:

> Cassandra, your eyes are like tigers,
>   with no word written in them
> You also have I carried to nowhere
>   to an ill house and there is
>   no end to the journey.
>
> *(ll. 6–10)*

Those wonderful lines on Cassandra trail off into a dark hint that 'There are those who did not want / it to come to an end'. That line leaves us hovering on the final word, and a wider than usual blank space is left before the next line begins; but it begins with a connective 'and'. The effect suggests that there is a link between the two elements – 'and' – yet that a type of distancing is taking place, a setting in perspective. This is what the following 'Del Cossa' lines achieve, as we shall see. The hiatus at the end of line 16 neatly catches the effect of a thought that has just crossed the mind, which then crystallises in

Their green does not swear at the landscape

The negro trainees – their uniforms green – who are part of the camp in which this criminal 'pax mundi' has landed the poet, remind him, in their attitudes, of figures in the Del Cossa frescoes in the Palazzo Schifanoia at Ferrara. Those frescoes were important to Pound and he told Yeats[4] how their construction gave him a useful hint for the structure of *The Cantos*. The frescoes are divided into three horizontal layers, and each separate section depicts a calendar month. At the top are divine beings, gods, goddesses: the Eternal. Below are the signs of the Zodiac: the Recurrent. At the bottom are depicted events at Ferrara in or around the court of Borso d'Este: the Transient. This can be pressed into very schematic use for analysing *The Cantos*, but like all such schemes it is of limited applicability. For instance, the negro trainees who look so like the figures of Del Cossa would correspond to figures in the bottom panel and hence be part of the mere flux of historical events. They are that, of course, but is there not in the present context another, more flexible possibility as well? Surely the juxtaposition of the Del Cossa reference to what precedes and follows it is a way of hinting that in spite of everything there is a scale of things in the cosmos, a design; and that art like Del Cossa's, based on the correct intuition of such a design, helps us in turn to grasp it: 'Their green does not swear at the landscape' echoes 'Learn of the green world what can be thy place' (Canto 81). The ending of Canto 77 substantiates this point in its reference to 'men move to scale as in Del Cossa's insets'. (I take '2 months' life in 4 colours' (Canto 78, l. 18) to be saying that art, as well as making us aware of scale and design in the cosmos, also condenses things to their essentials.)

The Del Cossa allusion has flanking contrasts in the preceding reference to the sinister machination of usurious warmongers ('There are those who did not want / it to come to an end') and in the following reference to a line adapted from Horace:

ter flebiliter: Ityn*

(l. 19)

* 'thrice tearfully [lamenting over] Itys'.

That line evokes a particularly brutal story of senseless passion from Greek myth, in which the protagonists were markedly lacking in a sense of scale and perspective. (Procne murdered her son Itys – Itylus – to avenge her husband Tereus' rape of her sister Philomela. Transformed to a swallow she laments her son: 'Ityn flebiliter gemens', Horace, *Odes*, IV. xii.) Hard upon this comes an effectively savage and ironical re-introduction of the 'pax mundi' theme. To close the temple of 'Janus bifronte' in ancient Rome was a token of the coming of peace: yet Janus was always depicted as facing two ways – 'two-faced' – and this allows Pound to register again his belief that the 'pax mundi' of 1945 was a travesty: just the kind of peace that would be contrived when world affairs were dominated by the kind of person who figures in the next vignette:

> 'and the economic war has begun'
>> Napoleon wath a goodth man, it took uth
>> 20 yearth to crwuth him
> it will not take uth 20 years to crwuth Mussolini'
>> as was remarked in via Balbo by the Imperial
>>> Chemicals
> its brother
>
> (*ll*. 22–7)

That is the kind of *obiter dictum* which Pound relishes for his epic, 'a poem containing history'. As Carne-Ross so valuably reminds us, 'it is a cardinal principle of the poem that the materials it presents must be presented exactly as they are or were. A man's actual words, and as far as possible even the sound of his words, must be reported, the date, location, etc., must be given. As Pound sees it, this is part of the *evidence*.'[5] Reference to Pound's prose-work *A Visiting Card*, published first in Italian in 1942, illustrates the point Carne-Ross has made:

> Let them erect a commemorative urinal to Mond, whose brother said in the year of Sanctions:
>
>> 'Napoleon wath a goodth man, it took uth
>> 20 yearth to crwuth him;

> it will not take uth 20 years to crwuth Mussolini'
>
> adding as an afterthought
>
> 'and the economic war has begun.'
>
> I know that drawing-room; that sofa where sat the
> brother of Imperial Chemicals. I know it. It is not
> something I read in some newspaper or other; I know
> it by direct account.[6]

'Sanctions', of course, refers to the League of Nations action against Mussolini's invasion of Abyssinia in 1936; and of Mussolini there will be much more to say very shortly.

Prior to Mussolini's emergence at line 36, however, Pound juxtaposes to the modern commercial and political malpractice we have just seen something comparable from fifteenth-century Italy: an instance of the poet's near-obsession with subsuming transient individual actions under a common pattern of recurrence. Piero di Medici had been betrayed by a commercial rival into an injudicious withdrawal of funds and 'Firms failed as far off as Avignon'. The whole Medici role in the Italian Renaissance was touched on in Canto 21, where that very same line occurs, and we should remember that Pound's attitude to the Medici was more ambiguous than his attitude to the modern financial world. Of course the Medici were involved to some extent in the increasingly corrupt banking practices of the Renaissance (Cosimo's 'red leather note-book' registered the degree of his involvement), yet in a Lorenzo di Medici there emerged someone whose wealth was used up in generous artistic patronage and whose civilised and successful effort at conciliating a dangerous Neapolitan prince is implicitly contrasted with the kind of 'pax mundi' we were confronted with earlier ('pax Medicea / by his own talk in Naples, Lorenzo', l. 30). Furthermore, Pound's verse tells us, responsively tightening up as it does so, that it was

Lorenzo

who left lyrics inoltre

>   that men sing to this day
> 'alla terra abbandonata'
>   followed him Metastasio
>   *(ll. 31–5)*

'Alla terra abbandonata', 'to the forsaken earth': the full-throated Italian of (presumably) one of Lorenzo's lyrics provides Pound with a link for his next episode, concerning Mussolini and Fascism. Lorenzo di Medici was a creative or 'factive' ruler-figure; so too, for Pound, was Mussolini. That 'alla' of the lyric meshes with a phrase in Mussolini's programme for a revitalised Fascism, outlined at the Verona Party conference in 1943, when Mussolini established his new Italian Social Republic in Northern Italy, the Salò Republic, as it came to be known. It may seem a dry point to endow with such lyrical expansiveness

> 'alla' non 'della' in il Programma di Verona
>   *(l. 36)*

yet such things mattered tremendously to Pound then. ' "Alla" non "della" '⁷ was an instance of precise definition, clarity of focus. The stylistic cunning of the Duce in introducing the distinction was a sign of his grasp of the essential issues of man's right relation to the earth which he cultivates and on which he builds his dwelling. Though Mussolini had to forsake Rome he had not forsaken the essentials of his visionary mission to redeem the 'terra abbandonata' in a wider sense.

In what follows (ll. 38–45) Pound remembers nostalgically certain episodes of his life in the expiring months of Fascism, including his own flight to the north from Rome in 1943:

> and the water flowing away from that side of the lake
> is silent as never at Sirmio
>   under the arches
> Foresteria, Salò, Gardone
>   to dream the Republic.

That moment of stillness on Lake Garda, where Mussolini in exile set up his Republic of Salò, had carved its trace deeply in the poet's mind; variant versions occur in Cantos 74 and 76, and all doubtless evoke a visit Pound paid to the 'Foresteria', or hostel for visitors, in the course of his efforts to advise the Fascist authorities during that period. Though the lines just quoted evoke a moment from a period when Pound was still burning with Fascist activism, they have an inwardness and peace that may seem paradoxical in the context. It is a paradox, however, that takes us to the centre of Pound's career. All the frantic correspondence with politicians and economists, the 'Ez sez' articles, the explosive didacticism, were so many layers of noise around an inner core of silence and of light. The true Pound – the poet of Canto 49 – was a Taoist in spirit, notwithstanding his rudeness about Taoism in the 'China' Cantos; and what was deepest in his Confucianism was the Taoist element in it: 'The sage delighteth in water' (Canto 83). It is this paradox which makes his career so dramatic to contemplate, and the ten years' virtual silence at the end of his life a true catharsis.

At this point in Canto 78 the paradox is very intense, since the Taoist peace emerges in the course of a section that deals with a period of intense Fascist activism. Yet was it not in defeat that what was most valid in Pound's attachment to Fascism emerged? He had seen it as an attempt to embody a visionary ideal of perfection – to 'build the city of Deioce' – and, when it failed, its quality of visionary ideal remained uppermost. Even Mussolini was reading Plato again –

> to dream the Republic.

Next the poet is set thinking of the origins of Fascism in the rally at Piazza San Sepolchro in Milan in 1919 – there had been a 'Programma di San Sepolchro' as well as a 'Programma di Verona'; a church with its candles and reliquaries is drawn into the associative net and a quarter-century's faith crystallises in the wonderful line:

> lapped by the flame, amid ruin, la fede
>
> (*l.44*)

The poet's daughter in her memoirs reminds us of the exalted yet baseless hopes of that terrible period:

> Despite all this Babbo relentlessly kept working, like a lonely ant, fighting his own battle. He wrote articles for *Il Popolo d'Alessandria*, a paper of the new republic; a copy now and again reached me in Cortina. By the end of the year he had written Cantos 72 and 73 in Italian. He sent them to me as a gift for the Befana of 1945. Full of vigor and images, exalting his old friends F. T. Marinetti, the founder of the Futurist movement, who, true to himself and his 'interventism,' had gone to fight in Russia. And Admiral Ubaldo degli Uberti, whose phrase *chi muore oggi fa un affare* – untranslatable: dying today is a good bet – sums up the state of mind of the loyal Italians as defeat inevitably approached. Idealism and heroism were by no means all on the side of the partisans. Babbo was infected by a desperate fighting spirit and faith. It is hard these days to define that faith or that spirit; it no longer seems a component of the air one breathes.[8]

Mary de Rachewiltz's book also helps us to understand the climax of the following section (ll. 46–59) – the nearest approach to a 'strong story line' that we ever encounter in *The Pisan Cantos*! They depict Pound's pilgrimage on foot from Rome in September 1943, when the Allied armies were approaching, to Gais in the Tyrol region of Northern Italy, where his daughter was staying with her foster-parents, a German-speaking Tyrolean peasant family to whom Pound was known as 'Der Herr':

> 'Someone to take the blame if we slip up on it'   46
> Goedel's sleek head in the midst of it,
>   the man out of Naxos past Fara Sabina
> 'if you will stay for the night'
> 'it is true there is only one room for the lot of us'   50
> 'money is nothing'
> 'no, there is nothing to pay for that bread'
>   'nor for the minestra'

'Nothing left here but women'
        'Have lugged it this far, will keep it'
                              (il zaino)   55
            No, they will do nothing to you.
'Who *says* he is an American'
            a still form on the branda, Bologna
'Gruss Gott', 'Der Herr!' 'Tatile ist gekommen!'
            Slow lift of long banners   60
            Roma profugens Sabinorum in
                                      terras
and belt the citye quahr of nobil fame
      the lateyn peopil taken has their name
bringing his gods into Latium
                  saving the bricabrac   65
'Ere he his goddis brocht in Latio'
        'each one in the name'
in whom are the voices, keeping hand on the
                                      reins

Following hard upon the more intensely wrought
passages about Lake Garda and San Sepolchro, with their
characteristic trochaic/dactylic rhythms, that episode of the
journey from Rome to Gais is rendered in abrupt, fragmented shape, the actual words of those encountered on
the way being transcribed in an unvarnished English
equivalent of the Italian original. 'Someone to take the
blame if we slip up on it' (l. 46) provides the transition, its
cynical irresponsibility contrasting with 'la fede' of the
previous passage. We catch a glimpse of one Goedel, an
official in the English section of Rome Radio where Pound
had given the broadcasts that led to the accusation of
treason, the rather slippery quality of Goedel, with his
'sleek head', being juxtaposed to 'the man out of Naxos past
Fara Sabina' (l. 48). The latter phrase surely refers to Pound
himself, in his Dionysos persona, walking past Fara Sabina
near Rome on his journey toward the north of Italy, and
bearing his 'lares et penates' to the new holy city of the
Duce, where a shattering mixture of material disaster and
spiritual resurgence was eventually to be his lot.

The scraps of utterance that follow (ll. 49–58) tell their
own story of the journey ('zaino' is knapsack, 'branda' is

hammock). We should pause, however, on ' "money is nothing"/ "no, there is nothing to pay for that bread"/ "nor for the minestra" ': their simplicity is charged with a deep charity, and other passages in the poem cast light on that reference to bread,[9] which for Pound was a substance whose quality and availability was one touchstone of an economic order's right relationship to the sacred bases of life.

The flight passage culminates in ' "Gruss Gott", "Der Herr!" "Tatile ist gekommen" ', which in turn leads into 'Slow lift of long banners' (l. 60). (Pound had remembered the banners in the nearby town of Bruneck.) The density of the image, and the spondaic weight of the line, which have been prepared for by the sound value of 'a still form on the branda, Bologna' (l. 58), achieves a most skilful transition to what follows. The poet, having rendered the journey in all its fragmented reality, wants now to give it a mythical, archetypal dimension, as the imminent emergence of Aeneas shows us. The heraldic effect of that 'slow lift of long banners' achieves the transition and leads us to accept the coming transposition of events on to an epical, latinised plane; and it transforms what might seem a rout into a triumph:

Roma profugens Sabinorum in terras

(l. 61)

The journey was not only what it narrowly seemed, a transient historical event – things seldom are in *The Cantos* – but an analogue of the journey from Troy of Aeneas, who came *bringing with him his gods*.[10] And that is what Pound stresses. What was essential had not been lost by the poet when he went from Rome into the lands of the Sabines (one remembers that Fara Sabina reference earlier on), for he, like Mussolini, has retained the vision of the ideal in the midst of chaos. In Pound's case especially – for it is the poet in his Odysseus-Aeneas persona, not Mussolini, whom the concluding lines lead us to envisage – the equivalent of Aeneas' gods are certain permanent and enduring values epitomised in the life and work of three famous friends:

> Gaudier's word not blacked out
> >   nor old Hulme's, nor Wyndham's
> *Mana aboda.*
>
> >   *(ll. 69–71)*

The words '*Mana aboda*', associated in Rabbinic tradition with the dignity of labour – 'he who is productive so that the world's work might go on has a share in God's labour of creation'[11] – were also the title of a poem by T. E. Hulme. Hulme, the sculptor Gaudier-Brzeska, and Wyndham Lewis are chosen here to epitomise those with a hold on the essentials of artistic creation and hence on values that endure. The Hebraic allusion may, of course, have an ironic implication, since if we look at the context of the preceding Old Testament reference – 'each one in the name' (l. 67) – we see that the prophet Micah wrote: 'For all the people go forward, each in the name of its god; but we, we go forward in the name of Yahweh, our God, for ever and evermore' (4.5). Pound's God was never Yahweh, and with terse pride he conveys that his task has its own type of divine sanction, mysteriously pagan: 'in whom are the voices, keeping hand on the reins' (l. 68). Yet in spite of the possible irony of the Micah reference, given Pound's known views on the Old Testament and Jehovah, the climactic '*Mana aboda*' still makes an effect of simple concise dignity: Pound's Just City, 'now in the mind indestructible', is aptly glossed by the Hebraic notion of a task achieved. It is also quite a good touch for rendering the high priestly seriousness we associate with Aeneas in his devout journeying to found another sacred city.

Aeneas, analogue of Odysseus, is in turn an analogue of the poet himself, whose arrival at the Salò Republic is transformed by the exalted comparison into a journey of dedicated achievement. *The Cantos* are full of images of purposeful action in the careers of resourceful voyagers: they epitomise the poet's admiration for dynamic action and constructive achievement, whether in war, government, exploration, *virtù*, art or science. Further instances of such admiration which come to mind, other than Odysseus and Aeneas, are Sigismondo Malatesta, John Adams, Nicolo d'Este, Marco Polo, Hanno the Carthaginian,

Frobenius . . . Such figures variously exemplify a common archetype, and with that realisation I think we touch on something that will carry us some way. First let us briefly call to mind as well the female figures who appear to blend with one another in *The Cantos,* such as Helen of Troy, Eleanor of Aquitaine, Parisina d'Este . . . Not only persons, but places and stories too, have a tendency to share in some archetypal pattern. One thinks of the variants of the Sacred City scattered throughout *The Cantos:* Ecbatan, Wagadu, or the more detailed Byzantium of *Thrones.* There is also Pound's attraction to the paradigm-story, best summed up in the phrase 'Troy in Auvergnat', Canto 5, and taken up again in Canto 23, where the poet establishes a parallel between a story of passion and war in twelfth-century Provence and the better-known story of the Trojan War. All that I have been discussing was condensed by Kenner in the happy phrase, 'subject-rhymes', to define the process whereby *The Cantos* press through many contingent details toward the archetypal and the paradigmatic. And from this comes something which affects rather curiously the group of voyagers earlier mentioned, whose dynamic activities are means of constructive achievement in time: the poet's tendency to subsume them by analogy under one paradigmatic image of purposeful voyaging undermines their temporal individuality and freezes them in a single pattern which appears timeless. As Thomas Clark has written:

> Pound is dealing with all history, with universal
> patterns of thinking and acting: he takes these
> patterns to be ubiquitous and timeless, simul-
> taneously present to the poem-microcosm. In a world
> where everything exists at once, there can be no
> progression.[12]

Pound was an artist who from the start of his career was peculiarly sensitive to the range and variety of historical knowledge which the nineteenth century bequeathed to the twentieth. He tried in his epic – 'a poem including history' – to overcome the random contingency of history by seeking through the very urgency of his historical sensibility to attain something akin to a timeless order. The opening section of Canto 78, with its culminating Pound/ Aeneas analogy, is a neat epitome of the whole process: the broken fragmented movement of the verse that describes the factual events of Pound's journey modulates into the hieratic rhythms of the redemptory Aeneas analogue. Confronted with what Mircea Eliade calls 'the terror of history' Pound strove through imagination to regain a lost paradise of timeless archetypes.

A passage of Eliade's *Aspects du Mythe* compares the vast effort of historical memory in the Occident in modern times to the way in which mythical events at the beginning of time are recalled in traditional societies. With all allowances made for important distinctions, he holds that both types of memory (*anamnesis*) 'project man outside his "historical moment". And a real historiographical memory also opens on to a primordial Time, a Time when men established their cultural patterns, in the belief that these patterns had been revealed to them by supernatural beings.' Those words may lead us to reflect on an earlier passage of the same book, where Eliade quotes from another author, J.-P. Vernant. It helps us to grasp something of the role of Odysseus in *The Cantos*, a poem in which the modern time-consciousness tries to regain contact with the realm of the sacred through the exercise of historical sensibility: 'J.-P. Vernant compares the inspiration of the poet to the calling forth of the dead from the world below, or to a "descensus ad inferos" undertaken by a living man to learn what he wants to know. The privilege which Mnemosyne confers upon the poet·is that of a contact with another world, the possibility of freely entering it and returning from it. *The past appears like a dimension of the Beyond.*'[13] That surely casts light on Odysseus. He functions in *The Cantos* not just as the most eminent of a group of constructive, ingenious and dynamic voyagers through time, all of whom tend to melt into one common timeless archetype. Odysseus is also the figure who, at the beginning of the poem, calls up the shades of the dead and thus establishes contact with 'the Beyond'; he is the hierophant of a religious rite as well as a purposeful voyager travelling, like the poet himself, through many times and places. The Odyssean descent to the realm of the dead at the

beginning of *The Cantos* has been associated with the
Eleusinian rites, which is a way of aligning the Odysseus
story with Dante's *Divine Comedy*: a journey into the depths
and up into the realms of heavenly light.[14] Pound's journey
through history, where stories, persons and events melt
into one another as avatars of various timeless archetypes,
thus becomes a kind of personal religious ritual whereby the
poet makes contact with the timeless realm of the sacred.
Imaginative re-creation of the past is a means not only of
reliving history but of transcending it as well. The poem
becomes its own 'artifice of eternity'. *The Cantos,* at times, lie
closer to the more mystical reaches of the Symbolist imagination than has been supposed.

These speculations could take us far, perhaps too far.
Eliade himself has been accused of giving a selective
account of what he calls traditional societies,[15] where
profane time has little meaning or importance and all efforts
are devoted to recovering through myth, ritual and symbol
a stable relationship with the sacred origins of the social
order. Yet Eliade, whether or not his investigations have
universal validity, has surely helped us to grasp one aspect
of *The Cantos*: possessed of an acutely sensitive modern
historical consciousness, the poet is nevertheless inclined to
collapse the contingencies of history into a number of
archetypal figures, paradigmatic actions and stories. Their
presence in *The Cantos* makes the poem seem like an intricate personal rite aimed at recovering the stability of the
eternal through a perception of the recurrent. The
rendering of such patterns of recurrence is one way in
which the poem hints at the existence of an encompassing
Process whose rhythms are cosmic and religious.

Yet to have said that is still to have missed the unique
quality of *The Cantos*. Described thus, it might seem that we
are dealing with a work of marmoreal stability, a series of
calm tableaux in which the random contingency of events is
lost from sight. The only section of the poem which does
have something of the effect of a hieratic 'tableau' is the
'China' Cantos, where the poet's imagination seems
content to rehearse, chronologically, cycles of decay and
renewal in lines which, for all their detailed use of historical
documents, have a beauty that is elegant but monotonous.

Much more typical of *The Cantos,* and especially of *The Pisan Cantos,* is surely the quality of fragmentation, discontinuity, the flux of the mind veering from one disconcerting segment to the next. The abandonment of chronological sequence might seem to encourage the effect earlier described, where a linear time-sequence of discrete historical events is collapsed into the mythical and the archetypal; and one cannot gainsay that that is partly the effect. Yet we come closer to the real nature of our response to *The Cantos* if we posit the existence of a three-fold effect which, at the cost of some slight repetition, I would describe as follows.

There is a sensibility ranging through a wide variety of historical material from many times and places, in which a journey, suggesting purposeful action and achievement in time, is intermittently prominent. There is denial of our expectations of chronology, as disparate events, persons, and actions fuse into archetypes and paradigms, which seem like attempts to recover the dimensions of the mythic and the timeless from the very contemplation of historical time; and this is linked to the poet's sophisticated fascination with myth itself, as a touchstone of religious vitality for passing judgment on the spiritual dessication of the present. Thirdly, and most crucially, the fragmented discontinuous mode of presentation introduces a chronically restless, inconclusive note: the stable, the recurrent, and the mythically timeless are being evoked by a temperament which is itself deeply time-bound, a creature of the flux, an *aficionado* of the contingent – as Wyndham Lewis and Yvor Winters well understood; a flickering, quicksilver, easily disorientated sensibility obsessed by ideals of stable clarity and ritual permanence. Hence we may well feel that the positing of timeless archetypes, paradigms and myths in *The Cantos* has the quality of aspiration rather than achievement: the aspiration of a rootless epigone of genius shoring fragments of eternity against the ruins of the present. It is 'Eleusis in the wilds of a man's mind only', as Pound himself with moving self-knowledge once expressed it. Hence the elegiac note, the note of loss, which so insidiously pervades much of *The Cantos.*

Is not a good deal of what I have been suggesting crystallised in the opening passage of Canto 78? It is a passage notably fragmented and discontinuous, yet it seeks to universalise the poet's plight by introducing the Aeneas prototype, since a need for the stabilising paradigm is one essential aspect of Pound's quest for religious wholeness. Furthermore, in the very midst of that restless opening passage, we have the glimpsed peace of quiet waters elegiacally remembered:

> and the water flowing away from that side of the lake
> is silent as never at Sirmio
> > under the arches
> Foresteria, Salò, Gardone
> > to dream the Republic.
>
> > > > *(ll. 38–42)*

In the contemplation of those waters the poet is drawn to write the phrase 'to dream the Republic': a vision of the ideal, essentially timeless, carved its trace in the mind amidst scenes of change, betrayal and chaos. Just as Hugh Kenner called Canto 49, the 'Seven Lakes' Canto, the still point of the whole series, so might one say that a recurring vision of water is the still centre of *The Pisan Cantos*.

3 The Waters of Memory

from the death cells in sight of Mt Taishan @ Pisa
as Fujiyama at Gardone
when the cat walked the top bar of the railing
and the water was still on the West side
flowing toward the Villa Catullo
where with sound ever moving
                           in diminutive poluphloisboios
in the stillness outlasting all wars
'La Donna' said Nicoletti
                           'la donna,
                                   la donna!'
                                   (Canto 74, p. 427)

                   said the Prefetto
as the cat walked the porch rail at Gardone
       the lake flowing away from that side
was still as is never in Sirmio
       with Fujiyama above it: 'la donna . . .'
               said the Prefect, in the silence
                                   (Canto 76, p. 458)

and the water flowing away from that side of the lake
is silent as never at Sirmio
               under the arches
Foresteria, Salò, Gardone
       to dream the Republic.

                                   (Canto 78, p. 478)

These three passages all relate to a single incident re-membered by the poet from his visits to Lake Garda during the days of Mussolini's Salò Republic in 1944, Nicoletti being then 'Prefetto' of the district. Lake Garda was one of Pound's sacred places ('who can look on that blue and not believe?') and the repeated evocation of this one scene gives it something of the status of an emblem: a man attentive to water, water that flows, yet specially held by that side of the lake which is most silent – the stillness of water. Water that audibly flows suggests the flux of experience; water that is still and silent causes us to suspend our passage through time in what Pound once called 'a contemplative fixation of thought'. The phrase comes from his essay on the sculptor Brancusi, where he writes of the fascination of crystal, whose contemplation has 'a sort of relation' to 'the contemplation of form or of formal beauty leading into the infinite', though inferior to the greater formal purity of marble.

Let us turn next to another memory of water where crystal itself plays a part.[1] It occurs in Canto 76, quite close to one of the three Lake Garda passages just quoted:

> Lay in soft grass by the cliff's edge
> with the sea 30 metres below this
> 　　　　and at hand's span, at cubit's reach moving,
> the crystalline, as inverse of water,
> 　　　　clear over rock-bed
>
> 　　　　　　　　　　*(Canto 76, p. 457)*

The poet sees through water a radiant purity that is never-theless tangible. To seek through water a tangible radiance which is the 'inverse' of water is surely akin in mood to being fascinated by the stillness and silence of water, water that nevertheless is ever-flowing. The common factor is a 'contemplative fixation of thought'.

Here is another passage on water which adds the con-templative associations of clouds to those of water:

> The Pisan clouds are undoubtedly various
> 　　　　and splendid as any I have seen since
> at Scudder's Falls on the Schuylkill
> 　　　　by which stream I seem to recall a feller

> settin' in a rudimentary shack doin' nawthin'
>   not fishin', just watchin' the water,
> a man of about forty-five
>
> nothing counts save the quality of the affection
>   *(Canto 77, p. 466)*

That water-gazing scene, remembered from youthful days in America, is juxtaposed to a slight variant of a line from one of the most well-known passages in *The Pisan Cantos*:

>   nothing matters but the quality
> of the affection—
> in the end—that has carved the trace in the mind
> dove sta memoria
>   *(Canto 76, p. 457)*

Thus contemplative gazing at water is associated with an allusion to a passage which stresses the power of memory to transcend the flux of time. The passage also contains a reference to the phrase 'dove sta memoria', from Cavalcanti's 'Donna mi priegha', translated by Pound as Canto 36.

Next let us think of a passage in Canto 74. In it the poet speaks of the carved trace of memory which survives the passage of time as *'formato locho'* ('formed trace') and as 'resurgent ΕΙΚΟΝΕΣ'. These phrases occur along with an evocation of 'La Nascita', Botticelli's Aphrodite, as she rises from the waves of the sea: she is a 'form beached under Helios', and often figures in *The Cantos* as the symbol of form elicited from the flux. The eyes of the goddess are compared to those of a woman greatly loved by the poet, Miss Olga Rudge; and the child's face is that of his daughter, Mary de Rachewiltz:

> her eyes as in 'La Nascita'
> whereas the child's face
> is at Capoquadri in the fresco square over the doorway
>   centre background
> the form beached under Helios
>   funge la purezza,

and that certain images be formed in the mind
to remain there
formato locho
Arachne mi porta fortuna
to remain there, resurgent ΕΙΚΟΝΕΣ

(Canto 74, p. 446)

'*Formato locho*' ('formed trace') in that passage, and 'dove sta memoria' ('where memory liveth') from the previous passage, are both talismanic phrases from Cavalcanti's 'Donna mi priegha', in which love draws strength from being based on a neo-Platonic philosophy of light. Hence Aphrodite is a 'form beached *under Helios*'. Memory, the light of the mind that retains carved images transcending the flux of experience, is also associated in that passage with a phrase from Pound's Italian version of the Confucian *Chung Yung*, 'Funge la purezza', whose English translation by the poet runs: 'the *unmixed* functions (in time and in space) without bourne. This unmixed is the tensile light, the Immaculata. There is no end to its action.'

The word 'Immaculata' occurs in one place only in *The Pisan Cantos*, along with an echo of that 'funge la purezza': at the climax of Canto 80 where Pound/Odysseus drowns in the waves of the sea, but is redeemed by the uttering of a strangely moving polyglot prayer, among whose elements is a reference to 'Immaculata'. Its Confucian light association seems to fuse with the more usual association of *Immaculata*, 'Immaculata Regina', a divinely redemptive female figure. In this confessional passage, Mary de Rachewiltz tells us, the poet is contritely remembering the unhappiness of his life at a period when the two women whom he loved, and who loved him, were in close hostile contact:

when the raft broke and the waters went over me,
Immaculata, Introibo
for those who drink of the bitterness
Perpetua, Agatha, Anastasia
saeculorum

repos donnez à cils
senza termine funge   Immaculata Regina

Les larmes que j'ai créées m'inondent*
Tard, très tard je t'ai connue, la Tristesse,†
I have been hard as youth sixty years

if calm be after tempest
that the ants seem to wobble
as the morning sun catches their shadows
(Canto 80, p. 513)

The incantatory act of confessional remembrance in that passage, directed upon divine female intercessors, rescues the poet from the turbulent waves of experience and re-establishes him (by the implication of the concluding three lines) in calm and in sun, much chastened. Might not one at this point remember that two of our three original passages describing the still, silent aspect of water concluded on a cry of

'La Donna' said Nicoletti
'la donna,
la donna!'
(Canto 74, p. 427)

The little episode retains its anecdotal vividness; probably Nicoletti with superb Italianate expressiveness did utter those words. Yet they have the unmistakable note of invocation, too.

The cluster of associations traced up to this point may be loosely summed up as follows: contemplation of the silent stillness of water, or of a radiance glimpsed through water; the power of contemplative memory to rescue what is loved from the flux of time – traces carved in the mind, *'formato locho'*, 'resurgent ΕΙΚΟΝΕΣ'; an image of Aphrodite rising from the waves, formed clarity from the flux; a living woman who is an avatar of the divine, invoked through memory, which is a kind of prayer. Let us next turn to a more extended passage from Canto 74, where some of these associations are present – a passage whose climax Mary de

* 'The tears I have caused drown me'.
† 'Late, very late, I have come to know you, Sadness'.

Rachewiltz associates with the poet's memory of her
mother, Olga Rudge:[2]

> ΧΑΡΙΤΕΣ possibly in the soft air
> with the mast held by the left hand
> in this air as of Kuanon
> enigma forgetting the times and seasons
> but this air brought her ashore a la marina   5
> with the great shell borne on the seawaves
>   nautilis biancastra
>   By no means an orderly Dantescan rising
> but as the winds veer
>   tira libeccio   10
> now Genji at Suma   , tira libeccio
>   as the winds veer and the raft is driven
>   and the voices , Tiro, Alcmene
>   with you is Europa nec casta Pasiphaë
>   Eurus, Apeliota as the winds veer
>   in periplum 15
> 'Io son la luna'. Cunizza
>   as the winds veer in periplum
> and from under the Rupe Tarpeia
> drunk with wine of the Castelli
> 'in the name of its god' 'Spiritus veni'   20
>   adveni / not to a schema
>   'is not for the young' said Arry,
>   stagirite
>   but as grass under Zephyrus
>   as the green blade under Apeliota
> Time is not, Time is the evil, beloved   25
> Beloved the hours βροδοδάκτυλος
>   as against the half-light of the window
>   with the sea beyond making horizon
> le contre-jour the line of the cameo
> profile 'to carve Achaia'   30
>   a dream passing over the face in the
>   half-light
>   Venere, Cytherea 'aut Rhodon'
>   vento ligure, veni
> 'beauty is difficult' sd/ Mr Beardsley
>   *(Canto 74, pp. 443–4)*[3]

The oblique reference in that passage to Odysseus adrift in the waves of the sea is an instance of the recurrent analogy made by the poet of *The Cantos* between himself in the turbulent flux of events and a hero-archetype. This is counterbalanced (ll. 3–7) by an image of Aphrodite rising on her shell from the sea-waves, her emergence blending with a mention of Kuanon, Chinese goddess of mercy, and with an allusion to Confucian reverence for the mysterious time-liness of organic Process.[4] The hieratic presence of Aphrodite withdraws with the same mysterious sudden-ness as it emerged, and we are then told this is 'By no means an orderly Dantescan rising': the poet stresses how fleeting are the glimpses of spiritual reality in a modern context where there is no 'Aquinas-map'.[5]

Instability is prominent in the ensuing lines (9–24), whose veering rhythms are beautifully suggestive of drift-ing and flux; yet, in counterpoint, certain hypnotic refrains and the invocation of sacred presences create the overall effect of a voice gently, insistently, intoning against the turbulence. Tossed now this way now that, no stable ascent; he can only plead: 'Spiritus veni'. He is passive in the flux, yet that passivity can be a kind of reverent waiting, 'as grass under the wind'. The flickering, unstable movement is token both of immersion in time and of the fact that 'only through time time is conquered'. This wind is also the wind of the spirit blowing where it listeth and suddenly 'Time is not', the moment of redemptive memory steals forth and a beloved face is posed in cameo-like stillness against the horizon of the sea:

> Time is not, Time is the evil, beloved
> Beloved the hours βροδοδάκτυλος
> >   as against the half-light of the window
> >   with the sea beyond making horizon
> le contre-jour the line of the cameo
> profile 'to carve Achaia'
> >   a dream passing over the face in the half-light
> >   Venere, Cytherea 'aut Rhodon'
> >   vento ligure, veni
> 'beauty is difficult' sd/ Mr Beardsley

(ll. 25–34)

Memory is light and rescues loved persons and things in momentary stillness. Such rescued forms are what we call beauty, and the reference to 'Cytherea' in those lines is both a tribute to the person who provoked this memory and a broader reference to Aphrodite as symbol of all formal beauty educed from the flux. But – 'beauty is difficult'. The tragic greatness of *The Pisan Cantos* lies in the completeness with which the poet conveys the disintegrating pressures of the flux of time, along with the spirit's winning of fragments of eternity from that very flux. These Cantos leave us with no unqualified affirmation; even the culminating visions of Cantos 81, 82 and 83 have subtleties of tone which elude finality. The ebb and flow of felt time, time the destroyer, is ingrained in the texture of the Pisan series. Yet in the very act of rendering the stream of consciousness in time the poet is also redeeming time, not only in the great moments, but in numerous little passing impressions and memories etched with that firmness of verbal outline so typical of his art. 'Amo ergo sum':

> But to set here the roads of France,
>   of Cahors, of Chalus,
>   the inn low by the river's edge,
> the poplars; to set here the roads of France
> Aubeterre, the quarried stone beyond Poitiers—
>   —as seen against Sergeant Beaucher's elegant
>   profile—
>   *(Canto 76, p. 455)*

>   So Salzburg reopens
>   lit a flame in my thought that the years
>   Amari—li   Am——ar—i—li!
> and her hair gone white   from the loss of him
>   and she not yet thirty.
>   *(Canto 79, p. 484)*

> And Margherita's voice was as clear as the notes of a
>   clavichord
> tending her rabbit hutch,
>   O Margaret of the seven griefs
> who hast entered the lotus
>   *(Canto 77, p. 471)*

Judith's junk shop
>with Théophile's arm chair
>one cd/ live in such an apartment
>>seeing the roofs of Paris
>>>>Ça s'appelle une
>>>>>mansarde
>>>>*(Canto 80, pp. 504–5)*

>and somebody's portrait of Rodenbach
>>with a background
as it might be L'Ile St Louis for serenity, under
>>>>Abélard's bridges
for those trees are Elysium
>for serenity
>>under Abélard's bridges   πάντα 'ρεῖ
for those trees are serenity
>>>>*(Canto 80, p. 512)*

Heraclitus's πάντα 'ρεῖ ('all things flow'), counterpointed against the still serenity of the adjacent lines, nicely epitomises the flux–contemplation duality so central in these Cantos. The fragments of the past recaptured in the quotations – all lovers of *The Pisan Cantos* will have their favourites, those are some of mine – have something of the quality which Proust sought through involuntary memory. Pound had no such theory of memory, and the velvety brooding of Proustian subjectivism was in any case alien to him. Yet the traumatic isolation of the camp, cutting off habitual responses, released a myriad tiny perceptions remembered in the gratuitous freshness of their timeless essences; and, as with Proust, it was often seemingly trivial things, holding themselves inviolate through the years against the deadening pressures of the practical intellect, which stimulated this kind of response. But whereas Proust constructed for himself in his great book a refuge of aesthetic isolation and self-sufficiency, Pound strikes one as being far more distracted and vulnerable. Things come to him in 'hints and guesses', not in the sinuous folds of Proustian syntax, let alone in orderly Dantescan revelations:

> Le Paradis n'est pas
> artificiel
>
> but spezzato* apparently
> it exists only in fragments unexpected excellent
>
> sausage,
> the smell of mint, for
> example,
> Ladro the night cat
> *(Canto 74, p. 438)*

The Pisan Cantos attempt a kind of self-therapy by verbal acts of memory and contemplation. Endemic to our response is the sneaking suspicion we have at times that the process is not always under the poet's control, as when he dwindles into mutter, or lunges into vituperation. At the very least our relationship with this poem must be allowed to be rather strange, due to its weird mingling of stylistic virtuosity with drift and fragmentation. (A nice example is the opening section of the famous 'lynx' chant in the latter part of Canto 79.) It is as if the poet were constantly re-forming a constantly dissolving self by a verbal mastery which is also a sequence of therapeutic ritual acts; the act of creative memory, in particular, being a kind of *mandala* for rescuing the self from the contingencies of time. 'Before any great task that begins a new life and calls upon untried resources of character, the need seems to arise for some introversion of the mind upon itself and upon its past – a plunging into the depths, to gain knowledge and power over self and destiny. It is, I think, of such an introversion that the underworld journey of Aeneas is symbolic. Such an experience initiation may also have been . . .' Thus Maud Bodkin, in *Archetypal Patterns in Poetry*. Her reference to the underworld journey of Aeneas can easily be transposed to Odysseus, Pound's main hero-archetype in *The Cantos*, and although Odysseus/Pound's voyage to the shades is, strictly, kept to the first Canto, one may surely see the Pisan experience, with its calling up of shades from the poet's personal past, as a variant on that theme; and the poem's occasional allusions to the sun's journey into dark-

---

* 'splintered'.

ness under the ocean reminds us also that the Odyssean story was seen by Pound as the myth of a solar hero, with a rhythm of submergence and resurrection. Furthermore, the recurrent references to the Eleusinian mysteries throughout *The Pisan Cantos* suggest that the series may be taken as a personal analogue of the initiation ceremony to which Maud Bodkin refers in her last sentence, especially if one recalls Leon Surette's theory that for Pound the Odyssean story had Eleusinian associations.

The Cantos as a whole, through acts of historical memory, tend toward collapsing the contingencies of history into paradigm and archetype, so as to attain in imagination a timeless condition akin to the recovery of sacred origins in traditional societies. In the Pisan series the poet by numerous acts of personal memory tries to reconstitute his fractured self, master his past, and attain a contemplative superiority to the flux of time: a kind of aesthetic eternity, whose emblem is that of a man drawn to the silent and still aspect of waters which nevertheless are ever-flowing. In both cases, however, the poet's sensibility honestly bears witness to the inherent desperateness of the undertaking. This can be seen in the jagged, nervy texture of so much of *The Cantos* as a whole; and in the Pisan series, especially, the sheer distraction of experience from which contemplative salvation must be wrung is communicated with painful truthfulness. Even some apparently simple affirmative utterances have an ambiguous quality. Take the lapidary comfort of these famous lines:

> nothing matters but the quality
> of the affection—
> in the end—that has carved the trace in the mind
> dove sta memoria
>
> *(Canto 76, p. 457)*

Surely the hint of a dying fall in the rhythm of those lines subtly conveys an impression of loss in the very act of affirming victory over time. This epitomises the ceaseless interplay in *The Pisan Cantos* between dissolution and inte-gration, form and chaos, as well as the elusive, sporadic fashion in which the poet renders the eternal, the formed,

the crystal seen through water. Notice with what effective
suddenness the latter vision is introduced at line 10 below in
the course of Canto 76:

and if theft be the main principle in government
   (every bank of discount J. Adams remarked)
there will be larceny on a minor pattern
a few camions, a stray packet of sugar
      and the effect of the movies   5
   the guard did not think that the Führer had
               started it
Sergeant XL thought that excess population
      demanded slaughter at intervals
    (as to the by whom . . .) Known as
          'The ripper'.

    Lay in soft grass by the cliff's edge   10
with the sea 30 metres below this
    and at hand's span, at cubit's reach
            moving,
the crystalline, as inverse of water,
   clear over rock-bed

    ac ferae familiares   15
the gemmed field *a destra* with fawn, with
            panther,
   corn flower, thistle and sword-flower
   to a half metre grass growth,
lay on the cliff's edge
     . . . nor is this yet *atasal*   20
   nor are here souls, nec personae
   neither here in hypostasis, this land is of
         Dione
and under her planet
   to Helia the long meadow with poplars
to κύπρις   25
   the mountain and shut garden of pear trees
          in flower
here rested.

        .   .   .   .

               (Canto 76, pp, 457–8)

The opening of the visionary section of that passage ('Lay in soft grass . . .') evokes an actual memory of glimpsed purity, of dream-like freshness, then modulates rather strangely into something hieratic and artificial, 'ferae familiares' being a verbal echo of the mysterious Dionysiac procession of Canto 20. Thereupon the whole preceding passage is deemed not yet '*atasal*', not yet a complete mystical union. Perhaps we should remember that in the essay on Brancusi quoted earlier the poet found crystal less efficacious as an image to suggest 'form or formal beauty leading into the infinite' than the sculptor's marble. The section closes with the poet's mind withdrawing into a consecrated dream of voluptuous purity:

> to Helia the long meadow with poplars
> to κύπρις
>   the mountain and shut garden of pear trees in
>   flower
> here rested.

       .   .   .   .

The strong pause marked by four dots reinforces the impression of a mind quietly closed in upon itself. Pear trees are traditionally symbols of fruitfulness and tranquillity of spirit.

The passage that now follows begins with an anecdote about a young Tyrolean peasant blinded near the end of the war, who returns to his own valley, the difficulties of the period being epitomised by the thin ribs of his cow: an abrupt recall to reality after the preceding visionary seclusion. Yet the anecdote's touching directness, suggestive of the simple pieties of rural life, does not completely break the flow of delicate spiritual hints that crowd upon the poet, since it adds a note of sadness and loss of the kind which frequently underlies his spiritual perceptions. Thus the anecdote casts a subtle poignancy over the ensuing 'wind out of Carrara', over the still waters of Lake Garda, and over 'La donna'; and all are coloured as well by the allusion to Dante's '*terzo cielo*', the section of Paradise where dwell those who greatly loved:

'both eyes, (the loss of) and to find someone
who talked his own dialect. We
talked of every boy and girl in the valley
but when he came back from leave
he was sad because he had been able to feel   5
all the ribs of his cow . . . .'
this wind out of Carrara
is soft as *un terzo cielo*
said the Prefetto
as the cat walked the porch rail at Gardone   10
the lake flowing away from that side
was still as is never in Sirmio
with Fujiyama above it: 'La donna . . .'
said the Prefect, in the silence

and the spring of their squeak-doll is
broken   15
and Bracken is out and the B.B.C. can lie
but at least a different bilge will come out of it
at least for a little, as is its nature
can continue, that is, to lie.

As a lone ant from a broken ant-hill   20
from the wreckage of Europe, ego scriptor.
The rain has fallen, the wind coming down
out of the mountain
Lucca, Forti dei Marmi, Berchthold after the
other one . . .
parts reassembled.

(Canto 76, pp. 458–9)

Across the vibrant stillness of contemplation and the
invocation of 'La donna' there breaks, at line 15 of the
passage just quoted, the harsh voice of the fanatic. Yet
although we might prefer it if Pound were to leave us on the
delicate fringes of religious mystery, it is part of the
authenticity of the Pisan series that he will not suppress the
disintegrating rage which he feels. Time the destroyer is as
strong as time the preserver. Pound's vituperative violence
is a curious strength, too, not something to be brushed
aside, tut-tutted over, hushed up. Religious visionaries,

even a rather complicated twentieth-century specimen like Pound, are not noted for their easy command of committee-room velleities. For Pound, Brendan Bracken, the BBC, and all they stood for were sheer evil. Evil is offset by fragments of silence and light. And light is the light of intelligence. It is lack of intelligence against which Pound rages, not sin. That is his break with the Christian tradition, and the reason why he loves Confucius and Mencius. His deepest notes may well be elegiac, but he never wholly despairs. 'The taint of the victim was not in him,' as A. D. Moody so well put it in his essay on Pound and Allen Upward, and the humorous pluckiness which emerges every now and again in *The Pisan Cantos* always brings up short any exclusive stress on the poet's elegiac qualities. Indeed, I suppose that the moral virtue which comes to mind first when reflecting on his character is: courage. Courage is there in the valiant gesture of 'ego scriptor' (l. 21), where he momentarily re-establishes the sense of his own exemplary role as a civilising light; but it is a role sustained amid wreckage, exposed to the elements, effortful: 'parts reassembled'. Then, with the same swift suddenness we noticed in an earlier visionary passage, an ascending radiance emerges:

> . . . and within the crystal, went up swift as
> Thetis
>
> in colour rose-blue before sunset
> and carmine and amber,
>
> spiriti questi? personae?
> tangibility by no means *atasal*   5
> but the crystal can be weighed in
> the hand
> formal and passing within the sphere: Thetis,
> Maya, Ἀφροδίτη,
>
> no overstroke
> no dolphin faster in moving   10
> nor the flying azure of the wing'd
> fish under Zoagli
> when he comes out into the air, living
> arrow.

and the clouds over the Pisan meadows
　　　　　are indubitably as fine as any to be
　　　　　　　　　　seen   *15*
from the peninsula
　　　　　οἱ βάρβαροι have not destroyed
　　　　　　　　　　them
　　　　　as they have Sigismundo's Temple
Divae Ixottae (and as to her effigy that was in
　　　　　　　　　Pisa?)
Ladder at swing jump as for a descent from
　　　　　　　　　the cross   *20*
O white-chested martin, God damn it,
　　　　　as no one else will carry a message,
say to La Cara: amo.

　　　Her bed-posts are of sapphire
　　　　　for this stone giveth sleep.   *25*

　　　　　and in spite of hoi barbaroi
　　　　　pervenche and a sort of dwarf
　　　　　　　　　morning-glory
　　　　　that knots in the grass, and a sort of
　　　　　　　　　buttercup
et sequelae

Le Paradis n'est pas artificiel   *30*
　　　States of mind are inexplicable to us.
　　　δακρύων　　　δακρύων　　　δακρύων
L.　　　P.　　　gli onesti
　　　　　　　J'ai eu pitié des autres
probablement pas assez, and at moments that
　　　　　　　suited my own convenience   *35*
　　　　　Le paradis n'est pas artificiel,
　　　　　　　l'enfer non plus.
　　　　　　　(*Canto 76, pp. 459–60*)

　　The mixture of esotericism and sensuous immediacy in
the first part of that passage is very typical of Pound in *The
Pisan Cantos*. The sunset glamour of lines 1–3 almost hints at
Shelley's skylark. The associations of a crystal sphere, the
Primum Mobile, are Dantesque; yet pagan goddesses,

Aphrodite prominent, inhabit the sphere of crystal. The tone of musing pedantry in 'spiriti questi? personae? / tangibility by no means *atasal*' (ll. 4–5), in which the poet records that this is not total mystical union (*'atasal'*), reminds us that we are reading a visionary poet who is also a scholarly dilettante of the twentieth century. Then the effortless precision and power of the lines on the dolphin and the flying-fish (9–13) seize the ineffable in the manner of a truly great poet.

Michael Shuldiner tells us that the description of the flying-fish as a 'living arrow' refers to 'the portrait of Christ as a living arrow. The picture is of a crossbow on which Christ rests like an arrow, ready to be shot heavenward, and can be found among medieval Christian icons'.[6] Our reactions to that explanation may well be mixed. Certainly the gloss adds something appropriate to the religious associations of the whole passage, thus making the image support another allusion to the Crucifixion a little later on (l. 20). Pound was not shy of letting drop allusions comparing his own situation to that of Christ, for to him Christ was primarily a symbol of death and rebirth, on a par with other myths of that type. Yet Shuldiner's gloss on the 'living arrow' risks giving it a fixity of meaning which blunts the impact of the poet's revelation of the vital universe itself – the flying-fish at Zoagli on the Rapallo coast whose leaping arc was perhaps recalled by the swooping movements of the 'white-chested martin' which is to carry a message to the woman, 'La Cara', whose love sustains the prisoner-poet (ll. 21–3). Perhaps it is worth noting that the arrow-like movements of a bird in flight also have Confucian associations for Pound, as we see from a passage in Canto 77 –

> nor does the martin against the tempest
> fly as in the calm air
> 'like an arrow, and under bad government
> like an arrow'

– where the last lines echo *Analects,* xv, 6, 1. Yet such matters have a way of blurring our response to a passage of beautifully relaxed power.

The flying-fish, the white-chested martin, the clouds

which 'hoi barbaroi' (Allied bombers) cannot destroy, along with the earlier hints of rapturous ascent in lines 1–3, all serve to render a spiritual essence: ascension, flight and freedom in that natural universe which for Pound, as for Wordsworth, was intrinsically holy; the 'world which is the world / Of all of us—the place where in the end / We find our happiness, or not at all'. Pound's use of Dante must be seen in the context of his own brand of 'Natural Supernaturalism' and not in any Christian context. The very last fragment[7] of *The Cantos* which Pound ever wrote begins:

> I have tried to write Paradise
> Do not move
>   Let the wind speak
>   that is paradise

This is profoundly Wordsworthian in sentiment, yet how much more fragile such things are in Pound than in Wordsworth, whose visionary dealings with the natural universe so often were held within the firm grip of a quasi-Miltonic syntax. By contrast much of the quality of Pound's best poetry in that vein lies in the way he seems to catch the fluctuations of the spirit on the wing, in all their uncontrived and intense mysteriousness.

Of course, Pound was fascinated by mystagogic symbolism and mythical patternings, and they are often very much there in the poetry, should we want them. After the poet has instructed the white-chested martin to 'say to La Cara: amo' (l. 23), he seems to withdraw into a hieratic trance:

> Her bed-posts are of sapphire
>   for this stone giveth sleep.
>
> *(ll. 24–5)*

Obviously the mystical properties of the sapphire excite legitimate speculation,[8] but it is surely the change of tone that makes the run of those lines so poetically effective, placed between the oddly shy urgency of 'say to La Cara: amo' and the casual unsought grace of the ensuing description of flowers:

> and in spite of hoi barbaroi
> pervenche and a sort of dwarf morning-glory
> that knots in the grass, and a sort of buttercup
> et sequelae
>
> *(ll. 26–9)*

Swift glancing perceptions dynamically interact to form imaginative wholes under the influence of a pervasive mood, yet each component of that mood is constantly asserting its own 'felt life'. This is poetry in which the reader has to be a co-creator, he 'must be always on his duty: he is surrounded with sensibility: it rises in every line', to adapt some words of Coleridge about Milton. When Pound says 'states of mind are inexplicable to us' (l. 31) we believe that he means it; there is not the contrived mystery of the type of symbolist poetry which is always ogling an allegorical gloss. Pound is truly open to tones of the spirit that for him truly exist in a world where 'it is not man / Made courage, or made order, or made grace'. Yet his perception of such things is 'not to a schema', it is 'spezzato', it is not 'an orderly Dantescan rising'. These delicately fluctuating perceptions achieve a unique air of spontaneous definition, so that when the confessional moment comes (ll. 34–6) it seems to have the quality of sudden revelation and not of contrived climax. Each fleeting perception is a victory over chaos, yet we feel the chaos *in* the poetry at the very moment we are admiring the art which masters that chaos.

The juxtaposition of separate intensities, in such a passage as we have been considering, is typical of much of Pound's best idiom in *The Pisan Cantos*. The poetry lives vigorously from moment to disjunct moment – a string of seemingly casual yet artfully moulded perceptions. Discontinuity gives a marked 'accent' to the perceptions as they pass; we are not allowed to subordinate one element to another in a conventional narrative or rhetorical *progression d'effet*. The poetry refuses to settle. But so intense is the cadence of each individual component that the effect of random improvisation is avoided. By eliminating the normal devices of progression or by giving connectives that do not in any obvious way connect – the presence of Pound's 'ands' can be as disconcerting as their absence –

the individual line or short section claims attention with hypnotic force. We are very aware of time as the medium of separate perceptions – the flux – yet equally aware of the timeless air of contemplation which distinct elements gain by virtue of their separation from what precedes and what follows. Total discontinuity is averted by associative links between the separate elliptical details, or by pointed juxta-positions which, once seized, make for an 'ideographic' type of illumination. And rhythm contributes an organic sustaining life of its own because it is not padded out with the normal aids to logical or rhetorical progression.

It is in rhythm and cadence, the qualities of poetry hardest to analyse satisfactorily, that Pound's great secret lies, as most critics have acknowledged. The voice weaves an unending *Sprechgesang* through fragments elliptically juxtaposed so as to induce in the reader a sense of their own strange unity: the hypnotic unity of a flowing meditation, in which echoes play, and eddies intermittently form, rather than a unity of development and climax – convenient though the latter word may be at certain points. Many of the extended sequences of *The Pisan Cantos* focus on the single line or phrase, that line or phrase having been given maximum effect by the often casual-seeming rhythms and cadences that precede it and in its turn exercising the subtlest of influences on what follows; so that a whole is contrived where the speaking voice has been musicalised but not distorted – an intricately sustained recitative where the want of a culminating aria is never felt, 'the movement of the voice rising, pausing, picking up, catching the phrase, and moving with it'.[9] Yet vocal line does not subordinate the elements of the composition to an over-riding rhythm; component lines or phrases retain, at focal points, their own carved integrity. This 'sculptured' quality, to use Donald Davie's analogy, retained amid the subtly modulated cadences of musical speech, is a special grace of Pound's work. So too is the swift change of register from elevated cadence to colloquial directness, the pared reticence, the sudden startling *cri de coeur*.

Any style bearing the powerful imprint of a personal rhythm will 'set up its own imaginative coherence, establish its own aesthetic normalcy', as Joseph Kerman remarked when discussing the atonal music of Schönberg and Alban Berg: 'Berg's opera is splendidly eclectic, undogmatic, inconsistent, and the powerful flux of style makes for his essential illusion.'[10] The essential illusion is exceedingly paradoxical in Pound's *Pisan Cantos*. They are intensely personal, 'confessional' poetry, yet highly sophisticated and stylised as well. Notable blendings of an urgent religious aspiration, in extreme personal circumstances, with highly stylised effects, will be touched on in the following chapter on Cantos 81, 82 and 83. As strange an effect of stylisation is to be seen in the great confessional outburst which occurs near the end of Canto 80, as prelude to the more expansive religious feeling of the following three Cantos. I have mentioned that confessional 'climax' at an earlier stage of the present chapter, but now wish to give it a rather different emphasis:

> when the raft broke and the waters went over me,
> Immaculata, Introibo
>   for those who drink of the bitterness
> Perpetua, Agatha, Anastasia
>   saeculorum
> repos donnez à cils
>   senza termine funge　Immaculata Regina
>   Les larmes que j'ai créées m'inondent
> Tard, très tard je t'ai connue, la Tristesse,
> I have been hard as youth sixty years
>   (*Canto 80, p. 513*)

The opening reference to Odysseus' plight in Book V of the *Odyssey* reminds us again of the importance of water throughout these Cantos. We think, too, perhaps, of the diverse symbolic associations of water. By its ceaseless flow it is an emblem of the destructive aspect of experience, the element in which we drown if there is no redemptive stillness, no radiance glimpsed in its depths. The avowal of 'Les larmes que j'ai créées m'inondent' takes up the drowning image and gives it a personal application. Yet waters can be redemptive as well as destructive; they have baptismal overtones; immersion in water is an act of lustration in many ancient cultures. Those healing aspects of water will gain prominence in the subsequent Canto 83: $'\upsilon\delta\omega\rho'$ 'HUDOR et Pax'. Eliot's phrase quoted earlier, 'only through time time is conquered', may be a helpful way of resolving the ambiguity of *The Pisan Cantos* water-symbolism, so prominent at the confessional climax of Canto 80. Mary de Rachewiltz draws attention to that climax in the following passage of her memoirs, associating it with the cry of 'Aoi' in Canto 81:

> And the cry of 'Aoi' is an outburst more personal than any other in the Cantos and expresses the stress of almost two years when he was pent up with two women who loved him, whom he loved, and who coldly hated each other. Whatever the civilised appearances, the polite behaviour and the façade in front of the world, their hatred and tension had permeated the house.
>
> > Les larmes que j'ai créées m'inondent
> > Tard, très tard je t'ai connue, la Tristesse,
> > I have been hard as youth sixty years
>
> Until then the attitude towards personal feelings had been somewhat Henry Jamesian: feelings are things other people have. One never spoke of them or showed them.[11]

The implication of Princess de Rachewiltz's comment is that the lines of Canto 80 are at long last an un–Henry Jamesian avowal of feeling. One partly agrees. The lines and the whole sequence in which they occur are certainly most moving. Yet surely there is something strange about the linguistic quality of this 'confessional' moment. For do not the lines in French endow anguished personal utterance with a hint of mellifluous 'distancing', a hint of reserve, in fact? The invocation of various Catholic saints, the reference to the opening stage of the Mass, the echo of Villon, the juxtaposing of 'Immaculata Regina' with 'senza termine funge' – a phrase associated with Confucian Light metaphysics and also used in an earlier Canto of Aphrodite when she rose from the sea, a radiant form from the flux – all

make for a passage of intense linguistic stylisation, whatever its content or message may be. It is made more so by
the sudden directness of 'I have been hard as youth sixty
years', which, placed against the muster of polyglot
invocations, is essentially an *artful* touch. By an incantatory
sequence of self-consciously eclectic gestures the poet
attains a markedly stylistic victory over experience as well as
a confessional catharsis. He is redeemed through ritualistic
utterance itself – *ex opere operato*. I feel something of the
same quality in Canto 74's 'Linus, Cletus, Clement'
passage, quoted in Chapter 1. Is it not the poet's art that is
saving him from the engulfing waves of time, language
itself becoming a kind of redemptive rite? Hence we may
find it oddly appropriate that this passage of confessional
catharsis in Canto 80 was directly preceded by a passage
attributing to the discovery of Professor Speare's anthology
of poetry a quality of redemption:

> That from the gates of death,
>   that from the gates of death: Whitman or Lovelace
>   found on the jo-house seat at that
> in a cheap edition! [and thanks to Professor Speare]
> hast'ou swum in a sea of air strip
>   through an aeon of nothingness,
> when the raft broke and the waters went over me,
> Immaculata, Introibo
>
> *(Canto 80, p. 513)*

Some words of Roland Barthes came to my mind when
trying to articulate the possibly excessive speculations of the
preceding paragraph:

> For modern poetry, since it must be distinguished
> from classical poetry and from any type of prose,
> destroys the spontaneously functional nature of
> language, and leaves standing only its lexical basis. It
> retains only the outward shape of relationships, their
> music, but not their reality. The Word shines forth
> above a line of relationships emptied of their content,
> grammar is bereft of its purpose, it becomes prosody
> and is no longer anything but an inflexion which lasts

only to present the Word. Connections are not
properly speaking abolished, they are merely reserved
areas, a parody of themselves, and this void is
necessary for the density of the Word to rise out of a
magic vacuum, like a sound and a sign devoid of
background, like 'fury and mystery'.[12]

Barthes's customary confusing brilliance surely conjures
up an atmosphere appropriate to the linguistic self-
consciousness and sophisticated artfulness of this 'confessional' poetry. And such reflections may do good in forcing
us to look in a new light at certain qualities of Cantos 81, 82
and 83, where the poet's sure instinct makes him render
with an oblique stylised subtlety the religious mysteries to
which he there draws close. This befits a poetry which,
eschewing the full-blooded visionary claims of Romanticism, still moves in that area of the numinous which the
Romantics attempted to re-formulate for modern times.
Pound, the cosmopolitan eclectic, wrote some of the most
authentic religious poetry of the twentieth century precisely
by virtue of his refusal to abjure the sophistication of a
cultivated man of the modern age. Yet he had enough of the
primitive and the *voyant* in him not to be drained of
religious vitality by his knowingness.

4 Rituals of the Self:
Cantos 81, 82 and 83

'A neo-Platonised Confucianism in which Eleusis figured as valid myth' – in those words of an earlier chapter I summed up the doctrine of *The Pisan Cantos*. It is not the kind of phrase likely to win fresh readers for Pound, and were it to do so it would be for the wrong reasons. On the one hand the neat formula sounds pretentiously arcane. On the other hand it seems to offer the spurious comfort of ideological clarity: *that*, for all their funny ways, is what the Cantos 'mean'. Yet Cantos 81, 82 and 83, in spite of being the climax of the Pisan series and the most impressive examples of the writer's powers at grips with the deepest matters, are curiously oblique in their handling of doctrinal issues. The Confucian 'Process', neo-Platonic light metaphysics, and Eleusinian myth are among the ingredients of the poetry, but they do not account for its peculiar effect and hence are not its meaning. The meaning must be sought in the form given to such ingredients by sharp contrasts of tone and by effects of deliberate stylisation which punctuate the seemingly random flux of the poet's soliloquising voice.

Pound may (or may not) have had a simple mind, but without any doubt he had an exceedingly complex and delicate sensibility. It was the mind, the top of the head, which made the stark affirmation: 'I believe the Ta Hio'.[1] The mind, angrily didactic, ground away in prose at economic theories of history and caused some of *The Cantos* to jerk out economic statistics like a faulty computer. Even the chastely carved rhetoric of the *Usura* Cantos may cause the uneasiness we feel with poetry which has 'too palpable a design upon us'. Certainly criticism of *The Cantos* is vitiated by seeking, and finding, too palpable a design and offering the reader a set of bracing certainties, such as this:

> Pound remains unshaken in his belief that 'there is something decent in the universe' . . . and if man will set aside selfish interest and take time and effort to see clearly, he will find the models of that decency . . . Ygdrasil, Castalia, the room in Poitiers, Eleusis and Arethusa are all sacred junctures of Heaven and earth, terrestrial loci of manifest process. Thus Paradise can be achieved if man, brought into harmony with the process, will seek out the eternal verities and permanent values that underlie all of life, especially in its cultural implications, and will manifest those truths in action.[2]

Admittedly Pound seems at times to invite such comment, but surely it does not quite catch the peculiar quality of *The Cantos*; and whatever be the case for a description of *Rock-Drill,* for *The Pisan Cantos* that note of rotarian uplift is downright misleading. It comes from an essay which, with impressive learning, traces the sources of Pound's allusions in *Rock-Drill* to the twelfth-century mystical theologian Richard of St Victor. But I wonder whether we are not taking Pound with the wrong kind of seriousness when we engage too pertinaciously in that kind of source-hunting. Take as an example the poet's use of the tag 'plura diafana' in Canto 83. It occurs in the course of an exquisite evocation of light and mist and water. The words have a remote, ethereal beauty of sound – a factor not to be underestimated when considering a poet's allusive phrases. We probably need to know that the phrase is a fleeting reference to the thirteenth-century Robert Grosseteste's writings on light, which have neo-Platonic bearings. And 'diafan' is usefully defined as follows: 'For we see light not by itself but in a certain subject, and this is the diafane.'[3] But what exactly is the nature of Pound's relationship to medieval culture? Scholarship that concerns

itself with the sources of his allusions may risk giving the
impression that the conceptual clarities and metaphysical
order of the medieval world are substantial possessions of
the poet. Precise definitions of matters physical and metaphysical such as one finds in medieval thought certainly
made a great appeal to him, as one sees, for instance, from
the well-known passage in his Cavalcanti essay where he
laments that 'we appear to have lost the radiant world
where one thought cuts through another with clean edge'.
Yet the paradoxical nature of Pound's relationship to such
clarity and order needs to be stressed as well. His own
sensibility, though precise and vivid in detail, was as a
whole turbulent and distracted, and his attraction to clear,
radiant and orderly world-views was essentially a Romantic
attraction. Hence 'plura diafana' in Canto 83, associated
with a cosmos of clear physical and metaphysical order,
standing isolated amid the poet's own fleeting and tenuous
epiphanies, carries a note almost of wistfulness.

Allusive phrases such as 'plura diafana', or even 'dove sta
memoria', seem to me like gestures towards an unattained
certitude and serenity, poignant precisely because they
occur in the veering course of an isolated modern consciousness. They evoke a nostalgia for systems of religious
and metaphysical wholeness: an aspiration, rather than an
achieved possession whose every implication in the source-
text we need to study with care. They are talismans, like
some of the Confucian ideograms that punctuate the text of
The Pisan Cantos; somewhat desperate symbols of the need
for cosmos in the midst of chaos, which illustrate the poet's
spiritual struggle rather than being tokens of his knowledgeable victory.[4] They are ingredients of the poetry, not
its meaning.

We are touching on the elusiveness of the religious
emotion that pervades *The Pisan Cantos,* even in Cantos 81,
82 and 83, which are its doctrinal climax. That emotion is
something exploratory, oblique, and refracted to us
through studied effects of stylisation. It moves crab-wise
towards the cosmic vision. Indeed, the achieved totality of
Romantic vision is dubiously appropriate to what the poet
undergoes, and the point at which he comes closest to
making a comprehensive visionary claim actually seems to

me a weak element in these three Cantos. I refer to the 'eyes'
passage, begun in Canto 81 and completed in Canto 83.
They are eyes associated with the divine and the sacred and
hence part of the mythological symbolism of *The Cantos*;
possibly they are also the remembered eyes of three women
whom Pound loved, as Wendy Flory recently suggested.[5]
Neither alternative affects my own view that the poetic
effect is flawed at its climax in Canto 83 in spite of the beauty
of the premonitory lines in Canto 81:

> Ed ascoltando al leggier mormorio
>> there came new subtlety of eyes into my tent,
> whether of spirit or hypostasis,
>> but what the blindfold hides
> or at carneval
>>> nor any pair showed anger
>> Saw but the eyes and stance between the eyes,
> colour, diastasis,
>> careless or unaware it had not the
>> whole tent's room
> nor was place for the full Εἰδὼς
> interpass, penetrate
>> casting but shade beyond the other lights
>>> sky's clear
>>> night's sea
>>> green of the mountain pool
>>> shone from the unmasked eyes in half-mask's
>>>> space.
>>> *(Canto 81, p. 520)*

This shows Pound's gift for mitigating a rather portentous
esotericism ('hypostasis . . . diastasis . . . full Εἰδὼς) by
delicate cadences and syntactic hesitations which suggest a
mind moving timorously, chastely, towards some rather
weird spiritual perception – a perception which is not 'the
full Εἰδὼς', not full contemplative union. Admittedly the
climactic evocation of the colour of the eyes has at best a
rather frail Imagist grace; but the final line expands marvel-
lously into the enigmatic.

The completion of the 'eyes' vision in Canto 83 is less
happy:

> A fat moon rises lop-sided over the mountain
> The eyes, this time my world,
>   But pass and look *from* mine
>   between my lids
>   sea, sky, and pool
>   alternate
>   pool, sky, sea
>
> *(Canto 83, p. 535)*

Here, where the highest reach of contemplation appears to be claimed with the spirit resolved into what it perceives, the effect seems to me obscure in a bad sense: not a legitimate refusal to indulge our hasty desire for full-throated visionary utterance, but rather a passage whose attenuated rhetorical patterning pretends to finality yet resists illumination. It has only a thin assertiveness.

If there is any justice in that view, the reasons for the flaw may nevertheless be interesting. Though religious in its essence, Pound's is not the kind of temperament which can any longer convincingly lay claim to the total visionary power of the Romantic. Yet he is not content to enclose himself in the hieratic subjectivism of the Symbolist, even though the rejection of sequential logic in most sections of *The Cantos* may remind us of one aspect of Symbolism. Pound in the Pisan series is still at his work of precise definition, 'chêng ming', paring away at inessentials so as to make manifest the vital energies of the real. He purports to look out on a real world, to re-create a historical past, to record traces of religious meaning in the universe that are no mere subjective imaginings. Yet, when at his most authentic, he still brings to the latter task his eclectic historicist temperament, his genius for oblique stylised effects, his twentieth-century feeling for the flux of experience. His stance is modern and subjective in that we are always conscious of Pound as a man who has to construct his own attitude to history, myth, religion; he cannot take for granted inherited patterns of response. Hence his most authentic renderings of the Holy, his approaches to Being, are refracted through a medium of twentieth-century anomie, and, in the very assertion of religious meaning, rhythm and tone may be hinting as well at loss, absence, distance.

The implied mention of Heidegger in that last sentence will have struck with added dismay the already over-burdened reader of Pound's poetry. Yet in thinking about *The Pisan Cantos* I could not help being drawn to Existentialist categories. If ever poet was in a 'Grenz-situation' Pound was that poet: alone, stripped of all possessions, threatened with the near-certainty of death. In such extreme situations the human existent (Dasein) is deprived of the inauthentic consolations of everyday talk (Gerede): things are no longer 'to hand' (Zuhandenes), available for use in the fulfilment of worldly projects; and the full implication of what it means 'to be' comes only in the realisation that one's being is a 'Being-Towards-Death' (Sein-zum-Tode). This need not be a doctrine of despair, or of the Absurd. Heidegger was misconstrued in that way on the basis of the early *Sein und Zeit*; later writings make – well, not clear – but seem to imply that his phenomenologi-cal account of human existence in *Sein und Zeit* was a preliminary to approaching what he calls Being. Being, in Heidegger's essays on the poet Hölderlin, is also called the Holy, and he ends an essay on *Hölderlin and the Essence of Poetry* by quoting a famous stanza from Hölderlin's *Brot und Wein* to exemplify the poignant situation of the poet in modern times:

> But Friend! we come too late. The gods are alive, it is
> > true,
> But up there above one's head in another world.
> Eternally they work there and seem to pay little heed
> To whether we live, so attentive are the Heavenly
> > Ones.
> For a weak vessel cannot always receive them,
> Only now and then does man endure divine
> > abundance.
> Life is a dream of them. But madness
> Helps, like slumber and strengthens need and night,
> Until heroes enough have grown in the iron cradle,
> Hearts like, as before, to the Heavenly in power
> Thundering they come. Meanwhile it often seems

> Better to sleep than to be thus without companions,
> To wait thus, and in the meantime what to do and say
> I know not, and what use are poets in a time of need?
> But, thou sayest, they are like the wine-god's holy
> > priests,
> Who go from land to land in the holy night.[6]

Such a passage strikes a thoroughly modern as opposed to a Romantic note, since it accepts the withdrawal of the gods, of the Holy. Yet it is not a passage of total despair. The poet still performs his mediating work, but in darkness, in 'the holy night'. And the reference to poets as 'the wine-god's holy priests' will of course not be lost on anyone who remembers Pound's fondness for Dionysos as a symbol of the sacred energies of the cosmos.

Turning to Pound in the light of this Heideggerian digression one can surely feel that all *The Pisan Cantos* show a religious temperament in quest of the Holy; yet, in token of the peculiar presence-in-absence of the Holy in modern times, a mood of elegiac distance subtly pervades their grasp of the religious. The poet caught that mood unforgettably in a few lines from one of the Last Fragments of *The Cantos*:

> The Gods have not returned. 'They have never left us.'
> They have not returned.
>
> > *(p. 787)*

In *The Pisan Cantos* the poet is plunged through the extremity of his plight into Heideggerian authenticity. Yet we shall see how, in Cantos 81, 82 and 83, poetic instinct and spiritual tact lead him to render his religious intimations in an oblique stylised manner, befitting the distance that must supervene in any dealings between so isolated and sophisticated a sensibility of the twentieth century and the realm of the sacred. It may even be that we shall sense the presence in those Cantos of an aesthetic attitude to the religious as much as the religious itself.

Let us now turn to those aspects of Cantos 81, 82 and 83 which may lend substance to the point of view I have adopted. Although it is difficult to determine structural fixed-points in so fluid a poetic medium, I think one can say that these three climactic Cantos are framed, in the first part of Canto 81 and at the end of Canto 83, by passages suggesting disillusion with worldly action and politics. Yet the whole opening section of Canto 81, down to the beginning of the *libretto,* is no mere record of despair, since it recalls things like the memory of a Spanish peasant woman's rough kindness, and a charitable negro's making of a table for the prisoner-poet, and also appreciatively evokes the philosopher Santayana's temperate acceptance of things and people for what they are. Such vignettes, however, stress private virtues and personal acts of kindness in a section whose mood is one of disillusionment with the hatreds, deceptions and pointless activism of the political world. It ends with the strange cry of 'Aoi' which, as Mary de Rachewiltz tells us,[7] records one of the deepest moments of personal loss and abandonment in *The Pisan Cantos:*

> AOI!
> a leaf in the current
>   at my grates no Althea

At this point, Canto 81 moves abruptly into a quite different register. A highly formal lyric in the seventeenth-century Cavalier mode cuts across the drifting despair of the preceding lines:

<u>*libretto*</u> Yet
Ere the season died a-cold
Borne upon a zephyr's shoulder
I rose through the aureate sky
                    Lawes and Jenkyns guard thy rest
                    Dolmetsch ever be thy guest,
Has he tempered the viol's wood
To enforce   both the grave   and the acute?
Has he curved us the bowl of the lute?
                    Lawes and Jenkyns guard thy rest
                    Dolmetsch ever be thy guest,
Hast 'ou fashioned so airy a mood
          To draw up leaf from the root?

> Hast 'ou found   a cloud   so light
>   As seemed neither mist nor shade?
>
>   Then resolve me, tell me aright
>   If Waller sang or Dowland
>   played.
>
>   Your eyen two wol sleye me sodenly
>   I may the beauté of hem nat susteyne
>
>   And for 180 years almost nothing.
>   *(Canto 81, pp. 519–20)*

With rapt solemnity this lyric, seemingly spoken by
Aphrodite, appears to affirm in its third stanza a tentative
hope that the poet's creations may not be unworthy to
evoke the ultimate mysteries of Being or, in Confucian
terms, the Process. After the lyric there is a pause; then the
eyes of a courtly love lady, evoked in Chaucer's own
fourteenth-century English, remind us that the eyes of a
goddess are one image of religious mystery in *The Cantos*.
Another pause; then an abrupt shift into a totally different
register:

> And for 180 years almost nothing.

That moody comment on the lack of any good poetry set
for music after the death of John Jenkins (1678), court
musician to Charles I and II, and with the birth of Arnold
Dolmetsch (1858) symbolising the possible revival of true
lyric,[8] pulls us back into the presence of a regretful, dis-
criminating connoisseur of the twentieth century. This
connoisseur is also a virtuoso at re-creating the lyric
measures of another age, as he has just demonstrated. He
has bodied forth for the reader, with conscious aplomb, a
creative relationship with what is valuable in the past; and
implied also, in the words of that re-creative act, is an
affirmation that such poetry is an expression of religious
mystery. Yet – and this is surely crucial – the calculated
artifice of the whole sequence is as marked as the moving
quality of the lyric itself. The poet goes out of his way to

draw our attention to the artifice by the line 'And for 180 years almost nothing', which is a device for distancing the lyric as well as the Chaucer quotation both from his own self and from the reader. The lyric gracefully ritualises Pound's sense of himself as an artist, which is obviously what redeems him from the despair of the previous section; and by the words of its last stanza it also hints at the religious mystery in which great art can participate. But the lyric's stylistic virtuosity, its prominence in the text as aesthetic gesture, establishes a certain distance between the poet and the mystery he is evoking, just as it distances the reader's response as well. This distance should not be seen as evasion or inadequacy. It is a kind of spiritual tact which enables Pound to put his stylistic virtuosity to the service of his awe at the mysteries contemplated. The artful rhetoric, and then the sudden change of tone, have the effect of establishing a remoteness from the religious wholeness craved. So too a hint of distance and loss is the silent companion of the exquisitely moulded cadences of this slightly later section of Canto 81:

> What thou lovest well remains,
> > the rest is dross
> What thou lov'st well shall not be reft from thee
> What thou lov'st well is thy true heritage
> Whose world, or mine or theirs
> > or is it of none?
> First came the seen, then thus the palpable
> > Elysium, though it were in the halls of hell,
> What thou lov'st well is thy true heritage
> What thou lov'st well shall not be reft from thee
>
> The ant's a centaur in his dragon world.
> Pull down thy vanity, it is not man
> Made courage, or made order, or made grace,
> > Pull down thy vanity, I say pull down.
> Learn of the green world what can be thy place
> In scaled invention or true artistry,
> Pull down thy vanity,
> > Paquin pull down!
> The green casque has outdone your elegance.

> 'Master thyself, then others shall thee beare'
> Pull down thy vanity
>
> *(Cantos 81, pp. 520–1)*

To call this parody or pastiche on account of its archaic mode is far too crude. It is wonderfully moving in its own right. The poet seems to be claiming to have exorcised Vanity through having seen what is man's limited place in the scale of a green world in which 'it is not man / Made courage, or made order, or made grace'. And there is an odd suggestion of the eighteenth century in the cosmos evoked; a Scale of Being that recalls Pope's *Essay on Man* as well as the Book of Ecclesiastes. The celebration of such a cosmos, in such an archaic mode, creates a slight gap between the reader and the religious insight conveyed. Hence the evocation of cosmic order has an undertone of remoteness in its assertions of consummated insight and possession. Moreover the assertion of cosmic order, in the latter part of the quotation, does not quite chime with the awestruck yet wistful agnosticism of earlier lines: 'Whose world, or mine or theirs / or is it of none?' These lines, placed amid the variously rendered 'What thou lovest well' refrains, augment a curious impression of sadness pervading the seeming assertion of spiritual triumph. The iterations have a dying fall. It is as if the poet is inventing as he goes along certain rituals for the articulation of his religious need, and these personal rituals carry an oblique hint of distance and loss in the estranging formality of their idiom. The refrains and the repetitions of ritual can also be a sophisticated means of inducing and sustaining religious emotions, and of this we shall shortly meet other examples.

The spiritual reserve of the poet, such as we have seen in Canto 81 – 'by indirections finding directions out' – emerges in another fashion in the famous 'Death' passage of the following Canto 82:[9]

> 'O troubled reflection
>   'O Throat, O throbbing heart'
> How drawn, O GEA TERRA,
>   what draws as thou drawest
>   till one sink into thee by an arm's
>   width   5

embracing thee. Drawest,
      truly thou drawest.
Wisdom lies next thee,
      simply, past metaphor.
Where I lie let the thyme rise   *10*
                        and basilicum
            let the herbs rise in April
                        abundant
By Ferrara was buried naked, fu Nicolo
      e di qua di la del Po,
wind: ʼἐμὸν τὸν ἄνδρα   *15*
lie into earth to the breast bone, to the left
                        shoulder
            Kipling suspected it
      to the height of ten inches or over
man, earth: two halves of the tally
but I will come out of this knowing no one   *20*
neither they me
                  connubium terrae   ἔφατα
                                    πόσις ἐμός
                  ΧΘΟΝΙΟΣ, mysterium
fluid ΧΘΟΝΟΣ o'erflowed me
      lay in the fluid ΧΘΟΝΟΣ;   *25*
            that lie
under the air's solidity
      drunk with ἸΧῺΡ of ΧΘΟΝΙΟΣ
            fluid ΧΘΟΝΟΣ strong as the
                        undertow
      of the wave receding   *30*
but that a man should live in that further terror,
                  and live
      the loneliness of death came upon me
                        (Canto 82, p. 526)

Here the two opening lines quoted from Whitman's 'Out of the cradle endlessly rocking' are the cry of the sea-bird lamenting his lost mate, and recall a boy watching and listening to the sound of a sea whose voice whispers Death. Walt Whitman's poem has all the expansiveness of Romantic poetry of vision and dream: nature, the sea, love and the loss of love are drawn together in an intuition of some great cosmic unity underlying birth and death. Pound too, as we know, was inclined to some such organicist vision of the universe in which all dualities are overcome, and that was one cause of his attraction to Confucianism. There is even an unexpected analogy to be found in Rilke's belief in the one cosmic process in which death is merely the 'other side' of life; and I was struck by the fact that J. B. Leishman, in his introduction to Rilke's *Sonnets to Orpheus,* alludes to a resemblance between Rilke's holistic vision and Confucianism by way of a quotation from Laurence Binyon's *Flight of the Dragon.*

Be all this as it may, one must surely be conscious of the special quality of Pound's handling of such matters. To move from Whitman's gloriously uninhibited *lamentoso* strains to Pound's terse notations is a little like coming to Webern after Wagner. Admittedly there is a degree of hypnotic repetition in 'drawn . . . draws . . . drawest'; he is slowly, delicately, chanting his *Liebestod.* Yet how moving is the affirmation of 'Wisdom lies next thee, / simply, past metaphor', its reticence conveying the poet's sense of the inadequacy of the word before ultimate religious mystery. The lines are a marvellous moment in *The Pisan Cantos.* Pound, so dominating and vehement, surprisingly refuses to claim autonomy for the imagination and is content to rest on a mystery which words can never encompass. Concerning the harmony of the total cosmic Process, the only paradise of which we know, the poet in one of the last fragments of *The Cantos* wrote: 'It coheres allright / even if my notes do not cohere.' His imaginative effort can seem incoherent and patchy, his greatness a matter of unco- ordinated intensities, if set beside other eminent 'modernists' like Valéry, Stevens, Yeats, Eliot: artists variously yet triumphantly enclosed in their own achieved subtleties. Also Pound never quite strikes me as a complex consciousness in the Jamesian fashion, but rather as a poet whose sophisticated sensibility and eclectic learning are always pressing towards central simplicity, a simplicity not of doctrine but of being. It would be idle to deny that his struggle along that path had elements of the chaotic. His 'errors and his wrecks' lay about him, as he put it at the end of his life; but, given the scope of the undertaking in *The*

Cantos, such 'failure' can be as inspiring to contemplate as the self-sufficiency of a more perfected *oeuvre*.

The realm of the sacred, whose essence has been rendered by a refusal to render – 'Wisdom lies next thee, / simply, past metaphor' – is next hinted at (ll. 10–20) by a sequence of fragments, allusive tessellations: an elegiac prospect of the living things that will grow from the body's earth: a reference to Nicolo d'Este, Renaissance ruler and lover of women, who asked to be buried naked in the loved earth; a hint of Theocritus' girl calling her lover back to her; a glance towards Kipling's poem 'The Wisdom of the Grave'; a gnomic allusion to Confucian non-duality. And then, quite suddenly – 'but I will come out of this knowing no one' (l. 20). We are back with an appalled desolate figure in a prison-camp in 1945, expecting the worst; and a similar effect occurs some ten lines later:

> the loneliness of death came upon me
>
> *(l. 32)*

Between those two tellingly stark reflections comes the 'ΧΘΟΝΟΣ' passage, in which the mistress-earth is transmuted into a fluid element (Whitman's sea that whispers 'death death death death death')

> fluid ΧΘΟΝΟΣ strong as the undertow
> of the wave receding
>
> *(ll. 29–30)*

Is it foolish to think at that point of Mauberley 'washed in the cobalts of oblivion'? I think not. *Si bene ponas ubique naufragium est.* All great poets are 'half in love with easeful death', and the sequence of 'ΧΘΟΝΟΣ' repetitions in this Canto show the poet inducing in himself, by a ritual refrain, an aesthetic attitude appropriate to love-death: not a love-death of Romantic abandon, but one tinged with the sophistication of a twentieth-century eclectic, who has come to the sacred by way of a Greece seen through the eyes of modern anthropology. He is easing the pain of solitude and despair by incantations that betoken a self-conscious imaginative participation in primitive religiosity. And in that personal ritual there is voluptuous release.

Release, relaxation, serenity of a kind, are the notes of much of Canto 83:

> one must count by the dawn star
>   Dryad, thy peace is like water
> There is September sun on the pools
>
> Plura diafana
>   Heliads lift the mist from the young
>   willows   5
> there is no base seen under Taishan
>   but the brightness of *'udor*   ὑδωρ
> the poplar tips float in brightness
> only the stockade posts stand
>
> And now the ants seem to stagger   10
>   as the dawn sun has trapped their
>   shadows,
> this breath wholly covers the mountains
>   it shines and divides
> it nourishes by its rectitude
> does no injury   15
> overstanding the earth it fills the nine fields
>   to heaven
>
> Boon companion to equity
>   it joins with the process
>   lacking it, there is inanition   20
>
> When the equities are gathered together
> as birds alighting
> it springeth up vital
>
> If deeds be not ensheaved and garnered in the
>   heart
> there is inanition   25
>
>   (have I perchance a debt to a man named
>   Clower)

that he eat of the barley corn
and move with the seed's breath

the sun as a golden eye
        between dark cloud and the mountain   *30*

'Non combaattere' said Giovanna
      meaning, as before stated, don't work
                  so hard

don't 勿
      助
      長

as it stands in the Kung-Sun Chow.
                    (Canto 83, pp. 530–2)

After the rapt yet relaxed movement of the opening lines of
that passage, with its yearning glance at neo-Platonic light
metaphysics ('plura diafana'), there is a slight but percep-
tible increase of formality in the phrasing from line 12
onwards and, as the passage progresses, a more archaic
diction. The poet is no longer simply contemplating, he has
gone on to ritualise his responses by means of a free para-
phrase of a passage of Mencius, pervaded by the Confucian
faith that the universe is a moral organism. It is the tone of
one who by ceremonial gestures is inducing in himself and
his readers an awareness of what such an attitude to the
universe is like. The question of 'sincerity' does not arise.
Pound is an imaginatively learned man attempting to
incorporate a remote religion into his own substance, and to
see through its eyes. All that counts is poetic effectiveness.
The undertaking is one in which an eclectic sensibility gives
appropriate stimulus to the religious imagination of an
eclectic age.

    The weird change of tone in the bracketed 'have I per-
chance a debt to a man named Clower?' (l. 26) brings us

sharply back to the solitary self of the prisoner in the camp, mulling over his memories. It is one of those little tonal shocks that Pound is continually giving us in the course of a highly artful 'stream of consciousness'. Thus when in the succeeding lines we assent to the Eleusinian and solar-myth overtones of eating barley corn and seeing the sun as a golden eye, we surely respond as well to the fragmentary placing of these perceptions on the page; this is myth mediated through the dramatic consciousness of a man whose sensibility is treading a delicate balance between despairing isolation and imaginative participation in mythic role-playing. *The Pisan Cantos* make fleeting allusions, for example, to the solar symbolism of the eucalyptus-pod picked up on the hillside path at Rapallo, when the 'partisans' arrested Pound in 1945; to the butterfly, emblem of immortal life, going out through the smoke-hole of his tent at Pisa; to the bone '*luz*', another esoteric symbol of resurrection. In addition, the recurrent imagery of moon and sun, so well described by Daniel Pearlman in *The Barb of Time*, may suggest to us that the whole Pisan series is a kind of mystical initiation culminating in the conjunction of sun and moon at a late stage of Canto 83, such a conjunction being known as an esoteric symbol of identification with the supreme good.[10] A legitimate question about this mystagogic symbolism in Pound is one that one is also tempted to ask about Yeats: how exactly did the poet take such matters, and how are we to take them? Whatever the precise status of Pound's beliefs, however, the poignant *effect* of such elements in *The Cantos* lies, to my mind, in one's awareness of an eclectic sensibility of the twentieth century using literary expression as a sophisticated private ritual so as to achieve a conviction of pervasive symbolic significance in the universe; such a conviction being a consoling feature of primitive religiosity as well as of the neo-Platonic and *Illuminé* tradition.

Some Pound criticism, however learned – because so learned? – seems to me to go astray by implying that the poetry is important on account of what it tells us rather than on account of the manner of its telling. Earl Wasserman's remark, quoted at an earlier stage, is worth repeating: 'the final goal of a critical reading is not to discover the universe in which the work functions, but the way in which it functions in that universe.' Of course mythology can be endlessly fascinating, and Pound himself was endlessly fascinated by it; but over-zealous critical pursuit of myth can make Pound seem like a version of George Eliot's Mr Casaubon who happens to have a penchant for versifying the notes of his 'Key to all Mythologies'. There is more excuse for this in some other Cantos, since they lack the unifying presence of a single dramatic consciousness which pervades the Pisan series. On account of that unifying presence much of the fascination of the series is to be found in odd shifts of tone and subtle exploratory stylisations of attitude, which fitly render the oblique course of a sophisticated spiritual Odyssey of the twentieth century.

A beautiful instance of Pound's methods is to be found in the following lines (31 ff.). He suddenly remembers a simple Venetian woman's humorous comment – 'Non combaattere', 'don't work so hard' – an implicit reminder perhaps, amid the timeless serenity that is now intermittently his, that too much of his life had been feverishly over-active. This leads, by way of some vigorous ideogrammic underlining, to an evocation of the happiness which the poet knew in Venice between the wars.

The Chinese ideographs glossing Giovanna's 'don't work so hard' –

勿

助

長

– mean 'don't make grow', and refer to an anecdote in Mencius admonishing those who try to bend the natural rhythms of the cosmic process to their own hasty desires. The effect of this direct allusion to the Chinese of Mencius, as it stands on the page of *The Pisan Cantos*, is to draw the reader by a kind of visual hypnosis – and perhaps the poet himself, for whom such ideograms had a talismanic appeal – into the secure orbit of Confucian wisdom, which confidently maintains that the universe is a living totality with its own serenely immanent laws. What a poignant contrast is thus achieved to the all-too-human sadness of the poet as he remembers his beautiful Venice:

> San Gregorio, San Trovaso
> Old Ziovan raced at seventy after his glories
>   and came in long last
> and the family eyes stayed the same Adriatic
>   for three generations (San Vio)
> and was, I suppose, last month the Redentore as usual
>
> Will I ever see the Giudecca again?
>   or the lights against it, Ca' Foscari, Ca' Giustinian
> or the Ca', as they say, of Desdemona
> or the two towers where are the cypress no more
>   or the boats moored off le Zattere
> or the north quai of the Sensaria   DAKRUŌN
>   ΔΑΚΡΥΩΝ
>
> and Brother Wasp is building a very neat house
>   *(Canto 83, p. 532)*

Yet in the very moment that DAKRUŌN ('weeping') evokes the unhappy depths of nostalgic memory, a new and more vital impulse is stealing into the mind, as the poet's eye alights on a wasp building its little mud-flask house on the top of his tent. Such a dialectic of feeling is very notable in *The Pisan Cantos*. There is so much rueful, tender, sharp-eyed love of things and places and people dead and gone, yet the sense of loss is always yielding to serenity because the very act of memory both preserves and renews. But that serenity may itself be tinged with sadness. Impossible to say which is uppermost. It is the elegiac mood *par excellence*.

There is nostalgia woven into the opening lines of the following passage, as the mind, awed by the constructive achievements of 'Brother Wasp', slips away for a moment from the tiny sanctities of the living universe in the present, back to Perugia, an Italian town dearly loved by the poet as an instance of human constructive powers and a place which, viewed from his present plight, seems a kind of *ville lointaine* of Romantic beauty. Then the haze of nostalgia dissolves as the memory of a cat's vigorous actions in the old suburb of Bulagaio in Perugia flicks his mind back again to the camp in the present, and to the surmised sexual prowess of Mr Walls, which in turn suggests the generation of little wasps, and new life. Here is the whole passage:

> and Brother Wasp is building a very neat house
> of four rooms, one shaped like a squat indian
> >   bottle
> La vespa, *la* vespa, mud, swallow system
> so that dreaming of Bracelonde and of Perugia
> and the great fountain in the Piazza
> or of old Bulagaio's cat that with a well timed leap
> >   could turn the lever-shaped door handle
> It comes over me that Mr Walls must be a ten-strike
> with the signorinas
> and in the warmth after chill sunrise
> an infant, green as new grass,
> has stuck its head or tip
> out of Madame La Vespa's bottle
> >   *(Canto 83, pp. 532–3)*

The short section which immediately follows (preceding another incantatory 'ΧΘΟΝΟΣ' passage based on the little wasp's descent into the earth) is well known, yet the final line is stranger and more elusive in its effect than has perhaps been realised:

> mint springs up again
> >   in spite of Jones' rodents
> as had the clover by the gorilla cage
> >   with a four-leaf
>
> When the mind swings by a grass-blade
> >   an ant's forefoot shall save you
> the clover leaf smells and tastes as its flower
> >   *(Canto 83, p. 533)*

The lines have all Pound's gift of seemingly casual notation, which gets things down with the minimum of rhetorical fuss, yet they are moulded with such cunning economy that art gets as close as it ever does to the immediacy of things. The poet, near to collapse, is saved by single-minded contemplation of the tiny energies around him, ending:

> the clover leaf smells and tastes as its flower

There is vital relish in that. There is also a kind of religious intentness – clover, perhaps, having paradisal associations for the poet, as mint had. But is there not also a hint of that quiet desperation we find in a Tennyson or a Rossetti, when they seem to try wresting the secrets of God or Nature by the hypnotic intensity of their sensuous contemplation? I think of Tennyson's 'Flower in the crannied wall', of Rossetti's woodspurge, 'the woodspurge has a cup of three':

> the clover leaf smells and tastes as its flower

It is like a man obsessively reciting words to himself as he gazes, and making the words a spell to exorcise unhappiness.

The note of a spell, a chant, is present in the 'ΧΘΟΝΟΣ' passage which follows, describing the little wasp's disappearance into the grass, seen as his descent into the Eleusinian earth to dwell with Persephone, with Tiresias . . . A passage so ravishing that the voice of the critic had better not be too much heard:

> The infant has descended,
> from mud on the tent roof to Tellus,
> like to like colour he goes amid grass-blades
> greeting them that dwell under XTHONOS
> ΧΘΟΝΟΣ
> OI ΧΘΟΝΙΟΙ;   to carry our news
> εἰς χθονίους   to them that dwell under the
> earth
> begotten of air, that shall sing in the bower
> of Kore,   Περσεφόνεια
> and have speech with Tiresias, Thebae

Cristo Re, Dio Sole

in about ½ a day she has made her adobe
(la vespa) the tiny mud-flask

and that day I wrote no further

There is fatigue deep as the grave.
(Canto 83, p. 533)

As with the earlier 'ΧΘΟΝΟΣ' chant in Canto 82, part of the
fascination of this passage is due to our sensing its
poignancy as the private ritual of a post-Frazerian eclectic,
who now draws Christ as sun-god into his syncretistic
mythologising. By the intoning of sacred presences the poet
is inducing in himself a trance. This is imaginative re-
creation of what it is like to have a religious emotion of a
pagan, chthonic type, rather than a direct visionary claim to
such experience. It is Eleusis in the wilds of a man's mind.
Pound's use of Greek in such passages is an attempt to
perpetuate a language valid for embodying the sacred, and
its strangeness on the page is perhaps a sign of that loss and
distance which the modern reader feels in the presence of
the poet's claim to be able to do so. The comment 'and that
day I wrote no further' (an adaptation of Francesca's remark
in the *Inferno,* Canto V) tells us of his own awe and exhaus-
tion of spirit as he stands back from the 'mysterium
tremendum' he has evoked through a personal ritual of the
imagination.

The relapse into despair that ensues is fleeting, and the
poet's humorous affectionate memory of Yeats's voice intoning during the composition of one of his poems mimics,
on a more humanly accessible level, the great generative
processes which Pound has evoked in the preceding
section. Throughout all three Cantos, there has been
recurrent stress on the importance of artistic creation and
the continuity of artistic tradition. The 'fine old eye' at the
end of Canto 81 was Wilfrid Scawen Blunt's eye, and
reminds us that Pound was one of a group of young poets
who paid a celebratory visit in 1914 to that conscientious
craftsman and independent spirit; Canto 82 recorded the

visit of the young Swinburne to the aged Landor, both poets
admired by Pound – and we may remember that when the
young Pound came to London he established contact with
every artist who mattered to him but, alas, 'Swinburne my
only miss'; and the opening of Canto 83 pointedly but
good-naturedly rebuked Yeats for being too prone to see the
symbol rather than the thing of beauty itself – a contrast
with Pound's own terse directness of vision:

> Le Paradis n'est pas artificiel
> and Uncle William dawdling around Notre Dame
> in search of whatever
>   paused to admire the symbol
> with Notre Dame standing inside it
> Whereas in St Etienne
>   or why not dei Miracoli:
> mermaids, that carving
>
> *(Canto 83, pp. 528–9)*

There is buoyancy and a noble confidence in all that
pertains to great art and great artists in *The Cantos*. Did not
Pound in some sense envisage even the religious wholeness
of the universe in aesthetic terms? To see the universe as
one harmonious organism of interpenetrating vital forces in
which there is 'no duality' is, in an extremely elevated
sense, to see the universe as a work of art, self-sustaining
and entire in itself. In politics, too, Pound admired the
'factive' personality who creates from dissident elements
some harmonious totality. In Cantos 81, 82 and 83 the
political element has been in abeyance as the poet creates
his own rituals of religious contemplation. The materials of
that religion may be ideologically eclectic, but their poetic
embodiment is singularly pure and authentic, intimating
with a fine elegiac tact the obscure intermingling of religious
wholeness with distance and loss:

> Down, Derry-down/
>   Oh let an old man rest.
>
> *(Canto 83, p. 536)*

Canto 84, which closes the Pisan series, strikes a different
note, and to it we must turn in conclusion.

5 Canto 84 and Conclusion

> Under white clouds, cielo di Pisa
> out of all this beauty something must *come*
> *(Canto 84, p. 539)*

Pound in his reading of Canto 84 on a Caedmon recording gives startling emphasis to the conclusion of those two lines:[1] the beauty of the Pisan sky – along with water so often the object of the poet's contemplative gaze – is now seen as an inspiration for actively realising the ideal order glimpsed by contemplation throughout the Pisan series. Coming after the weariness with political action expressed at the end of Canto 83, Canto 84's opening lament over J. P. Angold, a young poet-economist killed in the usurers' war, is a call to attention as well as an epitaph. Angold's death is embedded in a quotation from Bertran de Born's twelfth-century Provençal lament for Henry the Young King, elder brother to Richard Coeur de Lion; the Greek 'τέθνηκε' ('died') adds a further stern lapidary note:

> 8th October:
>> si tuit li dolh elh plor*
>>> Angold τέθνηκε
>> tuit lo pro, tuit lo best
>>> Angold τέθνηκε
>
> *(Canto 84, p. 537)*

* 'If all the grief and tears'.
† 'all the worth, all the good'.

Such waste should not go unavenged. Quietism was still, at this stage, alien to Pound's nature. Hence vignettes of action and dynamic enterprise pervade Canto 84. Pound's own voyage to America in 1939 is recalled, when he had hoped to see the President and stop the war, but encountered only Senators defeatist or cynical under the shadow of the hated Roosevelt:

> 'an' doan you think he chop an' change all the time
> stubborn az a mule, sah, stubborn as a MULE,
> got th' eastern idea about money'
> > Thus Senator Bankhead
> 'am sure I don't know what a man like you
> > would find to *do* here'
> > > said Senator Borah
> Thus the solons, in Washington,
> on the executive, and on the country, a.d. 1939
> > > > *(Canto 84, p. 537)*

A little later in Canto 84 we meet Carson the desert rat, an 'inventor'[2] who seemingly prospected in Africa and whose resilience makes of him a fleeting Odysseus analogue:

> and as Carson the desert rat said
> 'when we came out we had
> > 80 thousand dollars' worth'
> > > ('of experience')
> that was from mining
> > having spent their capital on equipment
> but not cal'lated the time for return
> > > > *(Canto 84, p. 538)*

Pound's great-aunt, who took him to Europe when he was young and she was old but still full of 'go', is another humorous image of human pluck and dynamism (like the remark of Pound's old friend Natalie Barney – 'Having got out of life, oh having got out of it perhaps more than it contained'):

> and my old great aunt did likewise
> with that too large hotel

    but at least she saw damn all Europe
        and rode on that mule in Tangiers
           and in general had a run for her money

like Natalie

        'perhaps more than was in it'
                  (Canto 84, p. 539)

Then (preceded by 'out of all this beauty something must come') we have a roll-call of Italian Fascist worthies and one or two others in France and Norway, which defiantly reminds us of where Pound had looked for the realisation of his ideals of economic justice and the good society. They are compared to three exemplary figures from Chinese history, and graded superior in the scales of Dantescan justice to the ever-adaptable financiers of a usurious capitalism, whose cause was abetted by that 'sputtering tank of nicotine and stale whisky', Winston Churchill. Hard to take, such sentiments, for a liberal of the West, especially for anyone who, directly or indirectly, really suffered in the Second World War. All the same, how glad one is that Pound did not conveniently renounce the cause he had supported, neither in his Pisan cage or tent nor in his madhouse cell in Washington. The intransigent old voice rings out on the Caedmon recording:

    Xaire* Alessandro
                Xaire Fernando, e il Capo,
    Pierre, Vidkun,
             Henriot
                    (Canto 84, p. 539)

Alessandro Pavolini and Fernando Mezzasoma were prominent Fascist officials in the North Italian Salò Republic, whither Pound journeyed in 1944 in the manner described near the beginning of Canto 78; Pierre Laval and Vidkun Quisling need no explanation; Henriot was the Vichy Minister of Information assassinated by the Resistance in 1944; and of course 'Il Capo' is Mussolini,

* 'Hail'.

present at the end of the Pisan series as he had been at the beginning, where his Fascist state was celebrated as a gallant attempt to realise the Just City:

> To build the city of Dioce whose terraces are the colour
> of stars.
> *(Canto 74, p. 425)*

A similar note is present in Canto 84, where all the vignettes of dynamic action and purposeful voyaging under the inspiration of an ideal are lyrically summed up in this passage:

> and as who passed the gorges between sheer cliffs
> as it might be by, is it the Garrone?
>   where one walks into Spagna
> that T'ao Ch'ien heard the old Dynasty's music
>   as it might be at the Peach-blossom Fountain
> where are smooth lawns with the clear stream
> between them, silver, dividing,
> *(Canto 84, p. 538)*

Such lines, placed in the midst of Canto 84's allusions to strife and injustice, as well as to voyaging and exploration, beautifully suggest that Pound was always seeking in the chaos of what we call reality for the realisation of a dream glimpsed through contemplation.

By neglecting the active, constructive and didactic elements of Pound's work, and by stressing its contemplative aspect and recurrent elegiac quality, I have in the course of this book risked implying a division which in the final analysis is unsatisfying. His love of the past, his reverence for all that was vitally beautiful in the natural universe, his admiration for all that was vigorous and pure in certain exemplary characters of human history, had the same source as his crusade for monetary justice, his zeal as an editor, his active devotion to the cause of great friends and contemporaries like Eliot and Joyce. That source was his passion for perfection, as Wyndham Lewis realised earlier and better than anyone else. Such love of perfection, of the ideal, characterised one who in essence was a contemplative, but whose prophetic vigour goaded him to realise his ideals in political action. For that he fought and suffered. If he was wrong in thinking such realisation of the ideal to be possible it was a generous, quixotic error. The violence of some of his writings, and a harshness of one side of his character, were the symptoms of an idealism frustrated. A more attractive expression of that frustration is the vein of sadness and loss that subtly pervades much of his greatest poetry and makes *The Cantos* elegiac in their essence, not epic. Yet that elegiac note arises from so radical a self-exposure to the destructiveness of time that it attains a seriousness transcending any minor connotations which the word 'elegiac' may possess:

> The enormous tragedy of the dream in the peasant's
> bent shoulders
>
> *(Canto 74, p. 425)*

It was the very same urge to perfection which drew Pound towards a *Weltanschauung* in which the universe is posited as a harmonious whole, where there is 'no duality', as he put it in his translation of the Confucian *Chung Yung*; and myths of fertility and light similarly manifest his aspiration towards religious wholeness where all dualities are subsumed by one underlying unity. For all his rejection of the more irresponsible aspects of Taoism, the deepest instincts of Pound's aesthetic and contemplative nature are surely best perceived through the doctrine of the Tao, as, for instance, one finds them so brilliantly rendered in the last book of Alan Watts.[3] And *Chung Yung (The Unwobbling Pivot)*, Pound's best translation from the Chinese, is significantly that one of the four Confucian classics which is closest in spirit to Taoism.

Yet, without impugning either the sincerity or even the validity of Pound's beliefs, the peculiar expressive poignancy of *The Cantos* can be said to lie in their making us aware of the restless, sophisticated eclecticism which was the necessary medium of this particular twentieth-century religious quest. The poet came to the deep springs of a mysteriously primitive religious feeling without attempting to suppress his ambiguous relationship to such matters. On the one hand this gives a certain abrasive tension to *The Cantos*, and on the other hand perhaps also accounts for the elegiac strain of distance and loss which permeates much of the work. 'And a modern Eleusis being possible in the wilds of a man's mind only?' Curiously enough it is the struggling, exploratory, 'imperfect' nature of *The Cantos* as a whole which may serve to make them germinal for the future, since they do not absorb one totally into their own imaginative self-sufficiency but set one on one's own path of intellectual and imaginative exploration. Viewed in that way even such rebarbative sections of *The Cantos* as deal with American history, for instance, can yield their own ambiguous rewards. Then Pound's greatness as a teacher, an instigator, finds its crowning, paradoxical fulfilment.

To say this is in no way to deny the artistic greatness of many separate portions of *The Cantos*. And of these separate portions *The Pisan Cantos* are perhaps the most notable sustained examples, since the terrible circumstances of their composition were the ideal precipitate of Pound's deepest imaginative powers. In them there is courage, humour, resilience; but ever and again a rhythm, a cadence brings 'the eternal note of sadness in'. If we read them with an ear for their tone, as well as for their rhythms and their cadences, they surely make us feel that the finalities of religion or of a religiously coloured vision of politics can only be realised in the solitude of the imagination – 'now in the mind indestructible', as Pound put it in Canto 74, quite close to a line which affirmed that 'the drama is wholly subjective'. *The Pisan Cantos* will remain his most moving single achievement, since they invest imagined harmonies and remembered perfections with the elegiac dignity of worldly failure. The strange silence which, after much further suffering, took possession of Pound near the end of his life can be seen not simply as remorse, a sense of defeat, but also as an intuitive awareness that what he had sought in life was beyond words as well as beyond realisation in action. Such awareness is desolating for the flesh but inwardly consoling for the spirit. A passage from Cyril Connolly provides the best, most chastening reflection for all who write on Pound, whether to condemn or to praise:

One would have to have something of Pound's greatness to judge him as he deserves: to assess the mixture of egotism and humility, genius and bigot, wit and warmth; the combination of technical virtuosity with lyrical insight. No poet has written so unfailingly well of water from the pagan springs of simplicity and wonder beneath his clear-eyed gaze.[4]

Notes

Introduction

1   A. O. Lovejoy, *The Great Chain of Being* (Harper & Row, Torchbooks, New York, 1960), pp. 293–4.

2   Taking a hint from Robert Langbaum's *The Poetry of Experience* (Chatto & Windus, London, 1957), p. 94: 'It can be said of the dramatic monologue generally that there is at work in it a consciousness, whether intellectual or historical, beyond what the speaker can lay claim to. This consciousness is the mark of the poet's projection into the poem; and is also the pole which attracts our projection, since we find in it the counterpart of our own consciousness.'

3   No man hath dared to write this thing as yet,
            And yet I know, how that the souls of all men great
            At times pass through us,
            And we are melted into them, and are not
            Save reflections of their souls.
            Thus am I Dante for a space and am
            One François Villon, ballad-lord and thief
            Or am such holy ones I may not write,
            Lest blasphemy be writ against my name;
            This for one instant and the flame is gone.

4   *Gaudier-Brzeska* (New Directions, New York, 1970), p. 85.

5   Ronald Bush gives a fascinating account of Pound's struggles to find an idiom that would encompass a variety of subject matter through 'masks', yet render adequately the peculiar note of a truly modern sensibility, in *The Genesis of Ezra Pound's Cantos* (Princeton University Press, 1975).

6   Robert Lowell in *Modern Poets on Poetry* ed. J. Scully (Fontana/Collins, London, 1966).

7   Richard Pevear, 'Notes on the Cantos of Ezra Pound', *Hudson Review*, 25, 1973.

8   W. N. Frohock, *South West Review*, XLIV, Summer 1959.

9 Hugh Kenner, *The Poetry of Ezra Pound* (New Directions, New York, 1974), p. 326.
10 Octavio Paz, *Children of the Mire* (Harvard University Press, 1974), p. 127.
11 V. Contino, *Ezra Pound in Italy* (Ivancich, Venice, 1970).
12 Conor Cruise O'Brien, *Writers and Politics* (Chatto & Windus, London, 1965), p. 143.
13 Contino, op. cit.
14 W. B. Yeats, *Essays and Introductions* (Macmillan, London, 1961), p. 526.

Chapter 1: General Considerations

1 Pound, *Guide to Kulchur* (Peter Owen, London, 1951), p. 135.
2 This phrase to describe incidents or characters that share in a common pattern or archetype is Hugh Kenner's, who has done more than any other critic to further the cause of Pound's work.
3 Pound, *Gaudier-Brzeska* (New Directions, New York, 1970), pp. 98, 125, 120.
4 Herbert Schneidau, *The Image and the Real* (Louisiana State University Press, 1968), p. 193.
5 Pound, *Guide to Kulchur*, p. 152.
6 Pound, of course, was well aware of these problems, e.g., 'The modern mind contains heteroclite elements. The past epos has succeeded when all or a great many of the answers were assumed, at least between author and audience, or a great mass of audience. The attempt in an experimental age is therefore rash' (*Paris Review*, 28, Summer/Fall 1962, p. 47).
7 *The Letters of Ezra Pound 1907–1941*, ed. D. Paige (Faber & Faber, London, 1951), p. 418.
8 Pound, *Guide to Kulchur*, p. 294. (For Pound, Eleusis was an important symbol of religious mystery.)
9 *Confucius: The Great Digest and The Unwobbling Pivot* (Translation and Commentary by Ezra Pound) (Peter Owen, London, 1968), pp. 179–83.
10 Pound, *Selected Prose*, ed. W. Cookson (Faber & Faber, London, 1973).
11 On this passage see A. D. Moody's 'Pound's Allen Upward', a brilliant example of Poundian exegesis (*Paideuma*, 4, 1975). Associated with the myth of Dionysos, according to Frazer, was a story of his having been cut to pieces by his enemies in the form of a bull.
12 I take the phrase from C. R. Dodds's introduction to Euripides' *Bacchae* since L. Littlefield tells us (*Paideuma*, 1, 1972, pp. 123–4) that the passage from which this phrase came was vigorously endorsed by Pound in his copy.
13 A. Miyake, 'Between Confucius and Eleusis: Ezra Pound's Assimilation of Chinese Culture in Writing Cantos I–LXXI' (unpublished PhD dissertation, Duke University, 1970). This remarkable piece of work is a detailed study of the synthesis of Confucianism, Eleusis and Scotus Erigena in Pound's outlook.

14 James Webb, *The Occult Establishment* (La Salle, Ill., 1976), pp. 108–13.

15 Miyake, op. cit.

16 Pound, 'Credo', *Front*, I, December 1930, p. 11.

17 Scotus Erigena in *Expositiones Super Ierarchian Caelesten S. Dionysii* (Migne, Column 128c). See on this topic P. Makin, 'Ezra Pound and Scotus Erigena' (*Comparative Literature Studies*, 10, 1973), and W. B. Michaels's 'Pound and Erigena' (*Paideuma*, 1 (I), 1972).

18 I think the simile in this passage from an uncollected essay by Pound may have a helpful bearing on *The Pisan Cantos*' mode of construction: 'We no longer think or need to think in terms of mono-linear logic, the sentence structure, subject, predicate object etc. We are as capable or almost as capable as the biologist of thinking thoughts that join like spokes in a wheel-hub, and that fuse in hyper-geometric amalgams' ('Epstein, Belgion and Meaning', *Criterion* IX (1930), 474–5).

19 Edwyn Bevan, *Symbolism and Belief* (Beacon Press, Boston, Mass., 1957), p. 134.

20 Barbara Charlesworth, 'The Tensile Light: A Study of Ezra Pound's Religion' (unpublished MA dissertation, University of Miami, 1957), pp. 84–5, 89.

21 S. M. Libera, 'Casting his Gods back into the NOUS', *Paideuma*, 2 (3), 1973.

22 Daniel Pearlman, *The Barb of Time* (Oxford University Press, New York, 1969), p. 290.

Chapter 2: The Heroic Paradigm

1 *Confucius: The Great Digest and The Unwobbling Pivot*, Translation and Commentary by Ezra Pound (Peter Owen, London, 1968), p. 20.

2 J. H. Edwards and W. W. Vasse, *Annotated Index to the Cantos of Ezra Pound* (University of California Press, 1971).

3 C. Seelye (ed.), *Charles Olson and Ezra Pound, An Encounter at St. Elizabeth's* (Grossman, New York, 1975), pp. 69–70.

4 W. B. Yeats, *A Vision* (Macmillan, London, 1962), pp. 4–5.

5 D. Carne-Ross, 'The Music of a Lost Dynasty', *Boston University Journal*, Winter 1972, p. 27.

6 Pound, *Selected Prose*, ed. W. Cookson (Faber & Faber, London, 1973), p. 283.

7 The whole text of section 15 of Il Programma di Verona is as follows (the point of the distinction is that there is not only a right of property on the part of all who have the wherewithal to acquire it, but a right to property guaranteed by the state to all the people): (15) 'Quello della casa non è soltanto un diritto di proprietà è un diritto alla proprietà. Il Partito inscrive nel suo programma la creazione di un Ente Nazionale per la Casa del Popolo, il quale, assorbendo l'Istituto esistente ed ampliandone al massimo l'azione, provvede a fornire in proprietà la casa alle famiglie di lavoratori di ogni categoria, mediante diretta costruzione di nuove abitazioni o graduale riscatto di quelle esistenti. In proposito è da affermare il principio generale che, una volta

rimborsato, il capitale pagato nel giusto frutto costituisce titolo di acquisto. Come primo compito l'Ente risolverà i problemi derivanti dalle distruzioni di guerra con la requisizione e la distribuzione di locali inutilizzati e con le costruzioni provvisorie.'

8 Mary de Rachewiltz, *Discretions* (Faber & Faber, London, 1971), p. 197.
9 See Carne-Ross's article for a brilliant account of 'come pan, nino' ('eat bread, me lad') at the beginning of Canto 81.
10 'bringing his gods into Latium. . ./ "Ere he his goddis brocht in Latio".' Pound brings into play the fifteenth-century Gavin Douglas's Middle Scots translation of the *Aeneid* which he so much admired.
11 I owe this gloss to a colleague, Mrs Frieda Kilov.
12 Thomas Clark, 'The Formal Structure of Pound's Cantos', *East-West Review*, 1, 1964, p. 108.
13 M. Eliade, *Aspects du Mythe* (Gallimard, 1963), pp. 171, 149–50 (my translation and italics).
14 Leon Surette has written a speculative, extremely fascinating article on these matters, 'A Light from Eleusis: Some Thoughts on Pound's Nekuia', in *Paideuma*, 3 (2), 1974.
15 Cf. J. A. Saliba, *'Homo Religiosus' in Mircea Eliade* (Brill, Leiden, 1976).

Chapter 3: The Waters of Memory

1 J. Cirlot's *Dictionary of Symbols* (Routledge & Kegan Paul, London, 1971) says of crystal: 'Like precious stones, it is a symbol of the spirit and of the intellect associated with spirit. It is interesting to note that mystic and surrealist alike share the same veneration for crystal. The "state of transparency" is defined as one of the most effective and beautiful conjunction of opposites: matter exists but it is as if it did not exist, because one can see through it. As an object of contemplation it offers neither hardness nor resistance nor suffering.'
2 Mary de Rachewiltz, *Discretions* (Faber & Faber, London, 1971), pp. 150–1.
3 *Line 1,* ΧΑΡΙΤΕΣ: the Graces. *Line 10, libeccio*: south-west wind. *Tira,* blows. *Line 11, Genji at Suma*: Noh play translated by Pound; the poet Waki awaits by the sea shore the appearance of the spirit, Genji – subject-rhyme with Oysseus awaiting rescue by celestial being. *Lines 13/14 Tiro, Alcmene . . . Europa . . . Pasiphaë*: mythological figures, all the recipients of divine visitation. *Line 15, Eurus, Apeliota*: east wind, south-east wind. *Line 16, 'Io son la luna'*: 'I am the moon', phrase used in *The Pisan Cantos* to identify Diana, the moon-goddess, and her silver crescent – the poet's Queen of Heaven. *Cunizza*: thirteenth-century lady beloved of Sordello; in old age freed her slaves; placed by Dante in Paradise – a member of Pound's compendious female pantheon. *Line 22, 'Arry, stagirite*: Aristotle! (denying the young's suitability for philosophy.) *Line 26, βροδοδάκτυλος*: 'rosy-fingered', Homeric epithet for the dawn, in this form a reference to Sappho's use of it for the moon. *Line 29, le contre-jour*: light coming from behind. *Line 30, 'to carve Achaia'*: having the perfection of Greek carving. *Line 32, Venere,*

Cytherea 'aut Rhodon': = Aphrodite ('aut Rhodon' still puzzles commentators). *Line 33, vento ligure, veni*: 'Come Ligurian breeze'.

4   *Chung Yung*: 'The master man's axe does not wobble. The man of true breed finds this centre in season, the small man's centre is rigid, he pays no attention to the times and seasons, precisely because he is a small man and lacking all reverence' (*Confucius*, Translation and Commentary by Ezra Pound, Peter Owen, London, 1968 (reprint), p. 103). The point of the line being that the resurgence of creative memory is an 'enigma' if one forgets 'the times and seasons' – but one doesn't.

5   *The Letters of Ezra Pound 1907–1941*, ed. D. Paige (Faber & Faber, London, 1951), p. 418.

6   Michael Shuldiner, 'Pound's Progress: The Pisan Cantos', *Paideuma*, 4, 1975.

7   This fragment appears in the New Directions edition as Canto 120. It is omitted in the Faber & Faber edition.

8   Michael Shuldiner (op. cit.) suggests that the lines can be clarified by reference to the Legend of Prester John, where sapphire bedposts have the associations of spiritual peace, chastity, and sanctioned procreation.

9   H. Schneidau, *The Image and the Real* (Louisiana State University Press, 1968), p. 193.

10 Joseph Kerman, *Opera and Drama* (Vintage Books, New York, 1956), p. 227.

11 Mary de Rachewiltz, op. cit., p. 258.

12 Roland Barthes, *Writing Degree Zero* (Jonathan Cape, London, 1967), pp. 52–3.

Chapter 4: Rituals of the Self: Cantos 81, 82 and 83

1   Pound, *Literary Essays* (Faber & Faber, London, 1954), p. 86.

2   D. J. Neault, 'Richard of St. Victor and Rock-Drill', *Paideuma*, 3 (2), 1974.

3   Albertus Magnus, quoted in J. J. Wilhelm, 'Guido Cavalcanti as a Mask for Ezra Pound', *PMLA*, 89 (2), March 1974.

4   '. . . the ideogram for Ezra was less an element of language than a mystical virtuous emblem to contemplate and get ideas from, like Yeats's Kabbalistic signs' (Hugh Kenner, 'D.P. Remembered', *Paideuma*, 2 (3), 1973). That remark of Dorothy Pound is not the last word on Pound and Chinese, but it has its interest.

5   Wendy S. Flory, 'The Tre Donne of the Pisan Cantos', *Paideuma*, 5 (1), 1975.

6   Quoted in Martin Heidegger's *Existence and Being* (ed. W. Brock) (Gateway Edition, 1967), pp. 290–1.

7   Mary de Rachewiltz, *Discretions* (Faber & Faber, London, 1971), p. 258.

8   This reading of the reference to '180 years' I owe to Peter Brooker's *A Student's Guide to the Selected Poems of Ezra Pound* (Faber & Faber, London, 1979), an excellent book which I discovered too late to be able to make as much use of as I should have wished.

9 Walter Baumann has a very learned and helpful commentary on each detail of this Canto in *The Rose in the Steel Dust* (Francke Verlag, Bern, 1967). I draw out merely those aspects of one passage of Canto 82 which fit the line of thought being developed.

10 J. E. Cirlot, *A Dictionary of Symbols* (Routledge & Kegan Paul, London, 1971), pp. 319–20.

Chapter 5: Canto 84 and Conclusion

1 Caedmon TC 1122 ('come' has been italicised by me, to reflect Pound's own stress).

2 Cf. *The Letters of Ezra Pound*, ed. D. Paige (Faber & Faber, London, 1951), p. 274.

3 Alan Watts, *Tao: The Watercourse Way* (Jonathan Cape, London, 1976).

4 Cyril Connolly, *The Evening Colonnade* (David Bruce & Watson, London, 1973), p. 274.

Select Bibliography

Works by Ezra Pound

The Cantos of Ezra Pound, Faber & Faber, London, 1975.
Personae, Faber & Faber, London, 1952.
Gaudier-Brzeska, New Directions, New York, 1970.
Guide to Kulchur, Peter Owen, London, 1951.
The Letters of Ezra Pound 1907–1941, ed. D. Paige, Faber & Faber, London, 1951.
Confucius: The Great Digest and The Unwobbling Pivot translations and commentary by Ezra Pound, Peter Owen, London, 1968.
Selected Prose, ed. W. Cookson, Faber & Faber, London, 1973.
Literary Essays, Faber & Faber, London, 1954.

Critical Works

Books

Barthes, R., *Writing Degree Zero*, Jonathan Cape, London, 1967.
Baumann, W., *The Rose in the Steel Dust*, Francke Verlag, Bern, 1967.
Bevan, E., *Symbolism and Belief*, Beacon Press, Boston, Mass., 1957.
Bodkin, M., *Archetypal Patterns in Poetry*, Oxford University Press, 1934.
Brooke-Rose, C., *A ZBC of Ezra Pound*, Faber & Faber, London, 1971.

Brooker, Peter, *A Student's Guide to the Selected Poems of Ezra Pound*, Faber & Faber, London, 1979.

Bush, R., *The Genesis of Ezra Pound's Cantos*, Princeton University Press, 1975.

Cirlot, J., *A Dictionary of Symbols*, Routledge & Kegan Paul, London, 1971.

Connolly, C., *The Evening Colonnade*, David Bruce & Watson, London, 1973.

Contino, V., *Ezra Pound in Italy*, Ivancich, Venice, 1970.

Davie, D., *Ezra Pound, Poet as Sculptor*, Routledge & Kegan Paul, London, 1965.

Davie, D., *Ezra Pound*, Fontana/ Collins, London, 1975.

Edwards, J. H., and Vasse, W. W., *Annotated Index to the Cantos of Ezra Pound*, University of California Press, 1957.

Eliade, M., *Aspects du Mythe*, Gallimard, Paris, 1963.

Eliade, M., *Cosmos and History*, Harper & Row Torchbooks, New York, 1959.

Hesse, E. (ed.), *New Approaches to Ezra Pound*, Faber & Faber, London, 1971.

Kenner, H., *The Poetry of Ezra Pound*, New Directions, New York, 1974.

Kenner, H., *The Pound Era*, Faber & Faber, London, 1972.

Kerman, J., *Opera and Drama*, Vintage Books, New York, 1956.

Langbaum, R., *The Poetry of Experience*, Chatto & Windus, London, 1957.

Lewis, Wyndham, *Time and Western Man*, Beacon Press, Boston, Mass., 1957.

Lovejoy, A. O., *The Great Chain of Being*, Harper & Row Torchbooks, New York, 1960.

O'Brien, C. C., *Writers and Politics*, Chatto & Windus, London, 1965.

Paz, O., *Children of the Mire*, Harvard University Press, 1974.

Pearlman, D., *The Barb of Time*, Oxford University Press, New York, 1969.

Rachewiltz, M. de, *Discretions*, Faber & Faber, London, 1971.

Saliba, J. A., *'Homo Religiosus' in Mircea Eliade*, Brill, Leiden, 1976.

Schneidau, H., *The Image and the Real*, Louisiana State University Press, 1968.

Scully, J. (ed.), *Modern Poets on Modern Poetry*, Collins, London, 1966.

Seelye, C. (ed.), *Charles Olson and Ezra Pound, An Encounter at St. Elizabeth's*, Grossman, New York, 1975.

Watts, A., *Tao: The Watercourse Way*, Jonathan Cape, London, 1976.

Webb, J., *The Occult Establishment*, La Salle, Ill., 1976.

Wilhelm, J. J., *The Later Poetry of Ezra Pound*, Walker, New York, 1977.

Winters, Y., *The Defence of Reason*, University of Denver Press, 1937.

Yeats, W. B., *Essays and Introductions*, Macmillan, London, 1961.

Yeats, W. B., *A Vision*, Macmillan, London, 1962.

Articles

Carne-Ross, D., 'The Music of a Lost Dynasty', *Boston University Journal*, Winter 1972.

Clark, T., 'The Formal Structure of Pound's Cantos', *East-West Review*, I, 1964.

Flory, W. S., 'The Tre Donne of the Pisan Cantos', *Paideuma*, 5 (1), 1975.

Frohock, W. N., 'The Revolt of Ezra Pound', *South West Review*, XLIV, Summer 1959.

Kenner, H., 'D.P. Remembered', *Paideuma*, 2 (3), 1973.

Libera, S. M., 'Casting his Gods back into the NOUS', *Paideuma*, 2 (3), 1973.

Makin, P., 'Ezra Pound and Scotus Erigena', *Comparative Literature Studies*, 10, 1973.

Michaels, W. B., 'Pound and Erigena', *Paideuma*, 1 (1), 1972.

Moody, A. D., 'Pound's Allen Upward', *Paideuma*, 4 (1), 1975.

Neault, D. J., 'Richard of St. Victor and Rock-Drill', *Paideuma*, 3, 1974.

Pevear, R., 'Notes on the Cantos of Ezra Pound', *Hudson Review*, 25, 1973.

Read, F., 'The Pattern of the Pisan Cantos', *Sewanee Review*, 65, 1957.

Shuldiner, M., 'Pound's Progress: The Pisan Cantos', *Paideuma*, 4 (1), 1975.

Surette, L. 'A Light from Eleusis: Some Thoughts on Pound's Nekuia', *Paideuma*, 3, 1974.

Terrell, C. F., 'The Na-Khi Documents I', *Paideuma*, 3, 1974.

Wilhelm, J. J., 'Guido Cavalcanti as a Mask for Ezra Pound', *PMLA*, 89 (2), 1974.

Unpublished PhD and MA Theses

Charlesworth, B., 'The Tensile Light: A Study of Ezra Pound's
Religion', MA dissertation, University of Miami, 1957.
Miyake, A., 'Between Confucius and Eleusis: Ezra Pound's
Assimilation of Chinese Culture in Writing Cantos I–LXXI;
doctoral thesis, Duke University, Durham North Carolina, 1970.
Fang, Achilles, 'Materials for the Study of Pound's Cantos',
doctoral thesis, Harvard University, 1958. (This work is an
invaluable source of purely factual information about *The Pisan
Cantos*.)

Index